the TOTAL Woman

Reflecting the Beauty of the Lord

CAROLYN HUNT

authorHOUSE®

AuthorHouse™
1663 Liberty Drive
Bloomington, IN 47403
www.authorhouse.com
Phone: 1-800-839-8640

Unless otherwise indicated, all Scripture quotations are taken from the King James Version of the Bible.

Published by AuthorHouse 3/27/2013

ISBN: 978-1-4817-1763-2 (sc)
ISBN: 978-1-4817-1762-5(hc)
ISBN: 978-1-4817-1761-8 (e)

Library of Congress Control Number: 2013903055

"Let the beauty of the Lord our God be upon us" (Psalm 90:17)

Dedication

To my Lord and Savior, words cannot articulate the magnitude of my love for you; and my gratitude for rescuing me from self-destruction and sending me on a journey to wholeness. Thank you dear Lord, for this life of wholeness which is far beyond anything this world had to offer. I am grateful for wholeness in spirit, soul and body. Without Your work in my life, I would not be. Thank you, Holy Spirit for your guidance.

This book is lovingly dedicated to the young ladies closest to my heart – my daughter, Shalonda Denise and my granddaughters; Lezli Denise and Sarah Danielle. You are a reflection of God's love and beauty. You bring me much joy!

To my sisters: Dr. H. Jean McEntire, Thelma L. Hendrix, Joyce F. Lewis, and Pamela Y. Sansome. I appreciate each of you for the kind of sister and ladies that you are. Each of you possesses special qualities and character traits like our mother. I love you!

To my sisters, who embraced me and opened the world of my father to me: Cynthia Jones McGee, Eunice Jones Darden, Wilma George and Willie Green, thank you.

To Velma Whitby, my spiritual daughter and friend, thank you for your creativity, the cover design and years of working with me to fulfill my purpose. I am grateful!

To all my spiritual daughters, the Daughters of Destiny at Walk in the Word Church, I appreciate and love you.

Acknowledgements

This book would not be possible without the love and support of…

Danny, my husband, friend, business partner, and yoke-fellow in Christ, you have been tremendously supportive and you've believed in me. Words cannot express my love and appreciation for you. I owe you big time, and it will be my pleasure to spend the rest of my life repaying my debt to you. The years have been terrific; I can hardly wait to see what else God is going to do through us.

Many thanks to my sister, friend and assistant in the ministry, Pastor Vivian Wade. Thank you for editing my work and helping me to put it all together. You are a jewel!

Table of Contents

Foreword

God is awesome! He is good! His desire is for each of us to be whole and complete – nothing missing, nothing lacking. He wants us to live in His blessings daily and to help us to do so He sent His Son, Jesus, so that we may have life and have it more abundantly. The author did an outstanding job of making a quality presentation of what it means to be a "total woman." She has not written from the premise of private revelation or human opinion but from the basis of the Word of God.

To understand the importance of being a total woman---whole, you must understand what is required to be transformed into a complete person in spirit, soul and body. The information and individuals discussed in this book give us a glimpse into the lives of those who bridged the gap and made the transition. This book gives a thorough and balance presentation of the importance and meaning of wholeness. I have hands on knowledge of Dr. Carolyn Hunt and her ministry. She is a woman of integrity and honesty. Carolyn has fellowshipped with different women and ministries who hold deep convictions about the meaning of a total woman—one that's submitted to God. Her approach to this issue is not from a legalistic point of view. Carolyn has one motivation: to help women become whole through greater knowledge of the Word of God.

She presents a wealth of insightful information and I believe that everyone who reads this book will be inspired to discover God's true meaning of a "total woman." Let me encourage you to read it with an open mind and a heart that is ready to receive. Ask the Holy Spirit to help you to receive God's divine thoughts concerning the subject. Like several other life issues, there are many references and examples in the Bible that makes it clear that God wants His daughters to be whole in every area of their lives. With confidence I can write a forward to this book because I believe what Carolyn is saying is right on! I believe the interpretations and applications contained in it are in line with Biblical truth. This book reveals the heart and mind of God. Women are God's masterpieces and He wants them to be complete in Him.

Being a "Total Woman" is a must for experiencing the fullness of Christ's blessings. God wants to chip away anything that hinders us from being beautiful! He wants us to be free from bondages and old wounds. This book will stir up your gifts and help lead you to your purpose. It will change your perspective and attitude about life as you look forward to reflecting the beauty of the Lord!

Dr. H. Jean McEntire
Founder of Word Alive Ministries, Inc.
Beauty for Ashes International Women's Ministry
Cincinnati, Ohio

Introduction

In this book, *The Total Woman*, I will share with you my journey to wholeness as well as provide some insight of the journey to becoming a "Total Woman." During my journey, I realized that there were many other women who were like me, who felt incomplete in certain areas of their lives and the lack of wholeness caused us much pain.

The Bible vividly describes the kind of woman God has designed us to be, Total! He created us to be whole in every area of our lives. But too often, we allow events and past experiences to define us. Our past seems to creep around our door and knock at our heart to keep it full of pain and regrets. Our journey of ups and downs should never determine who we are, but sometimes it does.

God created woman in His image to be a winner. Failure is never God's will for a woman who believes and trust in Him. He never wants her to succumb to defeat or lack. A life of insecurity and uncertainty are not a part of God's plan for you.

Doubt and fear is not in His menu. God created you with the potential for excellence. He has given us the key—the Bible, to unlock the treasure needed to be complete in every area of our life. Every woman, whether married, single, or divorced, or widowed can profit from reading this book and learning what God's Word says about being whole.

I have written this book to celebrate women by offering them encouragement and practical wisdom to being the "Total Woman." God created you whole from the beginning. It is my prayer that as you read through the pages of this book, you will open up God's treasure chest and discover everything you need to be whole and complete. Let's take the journey to recovering our original state. He has placed something within us to fill every place so there will be nothing missing in any area of our life. There is peace, purpose, power and prosperity in His wholeness. I DISCOVERED HIS TREASURE, YOU CAN TOO!

Chapter 1
A Journey to Wholeness

"And the very God of peace sanctify you wholly; and I pray God your whole spirit and soul and body be preserved blameless unto the coming of our Lord Jesus Christ" (I Thessalonians 5:23).

If you are woman who has picked up this book, wonderful, for you have just started on a journey to discover what it means to be whole. My journey was to search for answers to specific needs and desires in my life. It was a journey of discovering purpose and discovering the real me. I thought it would be a journey that would take a lifetime; but, when I embraced the journey, surrendered, and allowed God to do the work, it became enlightening and enjoyable. So get ready to take an excursion to wholeness. It is my sincere hope that you will forever cherish the trip.

Who Am I?

Through my years of ministry, I have discovered that many women have lost themselves in their seemingly over tasked every day duties and responsibilities. Many of them are realizing that they are not the woman they were called to be. Some of them have given themselves away to other people and do not realize that they are not whole. And many others never had the opportunity to discover who they are.

I know this journey all too well. I felt lost and incomplete for many years. My identity was completely wrapped up in things and someone else. I did not know who I really was or what I was called to do. I was lost and I did not know me. I can vividly remember when I first realized that I didn't have a true identity, I was thirty years old. I was going to school and caring for the home. I didn't work outside the home because my spouse made enough money to provide for us a comfortable lifestyle.

I was celebrating my thirtieth birthday. My mother and family and many of my close friends were all there celebrating with me. Everyone was laughing and eating and having a good time. All the gifts I desired were there. I stood on the back lawn, gazing into the sky, wondering what was wrong. Why was I so sad? I wasn't sure. Then I realized that the sadness did not come all of a sudden, but it had been ignored. Have you ever been in a crowd of people and felt alone? I did.

I realized that day that there was brokenness in my life. I was lost. I did not know myself. I was lonely with all my family there. I saw my life like a puzzle with some of the pieces missing. I felt like I was not really living my life but someone else life. But who was that someone. Answers would come later as I began my journey. This would be a journey to find self. I wasn't exactly sure what I was looking for, but I knew I needed to discover more about myself. I heard a preacher once say, *"We only have one self and you better know that one."*

Discovering Self

What are some of the things we do to find self? Some people change cities, change partners, attend another church, change careers, and buy a new car or home looking for their identity. Most of the time, all of these things are unsuccessful. I will share some of the things I did on the journey. I changed my dress style and colored my hair. I opened up my own business and changed my social circle. I changed schools and bought a sports car. Wow! None of it worked.

I heard another preacher say that "our lives should be well developed and balanced. It should be beautiful and standing strong." Well, that surely didn't describe me. Discovering ourselves is not found by searching outside of ourselves but searching from within. A lost self comes from within. When we don't have our true identity, we do not feel the connection with God. We know He exist, but not with us or in us. His presence is not obvious to us. We don't know His voice!

Sometimes we wonder if He even hears us or even cares about us! But, I would soon discover that only the right connection with our Heavenly Father will give us our true identity.

The Journey

To discover self I felt a good place to start would be at the beginning. How was I created and why? In reading and studying the scriptures, we discover that God was excited to create woman.

"And the LORD God formed man of the dust of the ground, and breathed into his nostrils the breath of life; and man became a living soul. And the LORD God planted a garden eastward in Eden; and there he put the man whom he had formed. And out of the ground made the LORD God to grow every tree that is pleasant to the sight, and good for food; the tree of life also in the midst of the garden, and the tree of knowledge of good and evil" (Genesis 2: 7-9).

I want to show you in scriptures the difference in the way God created man from woman.

Let's read further.

"And the LORD God took the man, and put him into the Garden of Eden to dress it and to keep it. And the LORD God commanded the man, saying, Of every tree of the garden thou mayest freely eat: But of the tree of the knowledge of good and evil, thou shalt not eat

of it: for in the day that thou eatest thereof thou shalt surely die. And the LORD God said, It is not good that the man should be alone; I will make him an help meet for him."

And out of the ground the LORD God formed every beast of the field, and every fowl of the air; and brought them unto Adam to see what he would call them: and whatsoever Adam called every living creature, that was the name thereof. And Adam gave names to all cattle, and to the fowl of the air, and to every beast of the field; but for Adam there was not found an help meet for him" (Genesis 2:15-20).

The scriptures tell us that God created the animals and beasts and told Adam to name each of them. WOW! Adam was a genius! He had the ability to name all the animals and beasts. Adam was God's masterpiece, but there was one problem. All the animals had a mate. God saw that there was not a helper or mate for Adam; one who was suitable and adaptable and who would complete him. God said that it was not good for man to be alone so He would make him a help mate. I like that word "make." It reminds me of designing a dress. Yes, that is what God did, he designed the woman!

"And the LORD God caused a deep sleep to fall upon Adam and he slept: and he took one of his ribs, and closed up the flesh instead thereof; And the rib, which the LORD God had taken from man, made he a woman, and brought her unto the man. And Adam said, This is now bone of my bones, and flesh of my flesh: she shall be called Woman, because she was taken out of Man. Therefore shall a man leave his father and his mother, and shall cleave unto his wife: and they shall be one flesh. And they were both naked, the man and his wife, and were not ashamed" (Genesis 2:21-25). Recognizing the difference between man and woman is important in knowing who we are.

God caused a deep sleep to fall on Adam and He took the rib from Adam, and made a woman and brought her to the man. When Adam woke up, he marveled at the beautiful creature next to him.   The Bible does not tell us about her physical appearance. It did not say if she was short or tall, fat or skinny! What it said was she was woman! **This gift was made and shaped into a unique fashion**. Women, you were made like nothing else.

God created everything BUT you! He prepared you in man!

You see, God took the muddy dirt from the ground, shaped it, and formed man. He breathed into it and it became man. In the original Hebrew, one definition for being formed is *"squeezed together."* I can see that, man was squeezed. But because the woman was very special – God kept her hidden within the man. He fashioned her, but He did not allow her to emerge until the entire creation process was completed.

In Genesis 2:12 the scripture says that God created woman. She was "skillfully and carefully handcrafted." **You are one of a kind!** There is nothing else on earth that is even close to being the creature that you are. Woman, you were designed with distinct characteristics. God designed you and destined you for purpose!

When you don't know whose you are and who you are, you will allow other people and things to define you! Knowing who you are is not about physical appearance! It is much more. Woman was taken from BONE, the bone of man, his rib, NOT EARTH. God made women to be lovely, gentle, clean and beautiful on the inside and outside. Women were fashioned to be strong in character – WE ARE BONE! We should be soft in our demeanor, countenance and appearance.

I wonder why God didn't just create woman the same way He did man. Why didn't He just scoop up some more mud and form woman just as He had the man? I believe He wanted woman to be whole and complete. Eve - the first woman who was shaped was whole! She was flawless and lived in a flawless world. She had it going on! She was free to be all that any woman could ever be. You name it, Eve was. When I see Eve, (before her decision to eat the fruit) I see what I was created to be, and what God's original plan for us was. **He wanted us to be TOTAL, whole and complete in every area**. He created us that way.

God wasn't satisfied that He had made Adam alone. He pulled woman out of Him so that Adam would be better than before. But Adam would be missing something, his rib. Women are special and significant! The woman was designed to be suitable, adaptable and made to complete him. God said she was his "help meet." In other words she was going to *help* him, which means "to be of assistance and to aid." The word, *meet* means "to come together and to surround." Woman was created to surround man and assist him. To be whole you have to know how you were created and to accept yourself as you were created. You need to know your design. You are *"fearfully and wonderfully made"* (Psalm 139:14).

What is Wholeness?

We often hear the word "wholeness." That's what this book is about, being whole, but what does it really mean? Given our fallen nature, can a person really become whole? Wholeness involves many different facets of a woman's life, the spiritual, the mental, the physical, the relational, the emotional, and the professional. There are so many facets to being a woman that sometimes we feel torn, separated and confused by our very own lives. We have many roles that we have to fill in our lives. As women, we wear many hats. We are wives, mothers, grandmothers, cooks, chauffeurs, church workers, professionals, and even hockey moms. We are multi-tasked and God equips us to fulfill each role. We can hold the baby on the hip, have a load of clothes in the washer, stir the food on the stove, answer Caleb's math question, and say yes honey it's in the back closet, all at the same time. But our lives must be balanced and that requires wholeness.

When any part of our lives is unhealthy, wounded, or incomplete, it affects the other parts. The total woman is affected.

As a woman, you have to learn to be balance and understand every area of your life. You have to connect the parts and evaluate them to see if each one is whole or if there are broken parts. To fulfill your destiny, you must know who you are and how each part of your life works together. All of you must be healed and made complete on the journey to wholeness. So if you are broken physically, emotionally or in any way allow God to heal you. It is His desire to make you whole that your life may be full and prosperous.

Lets' explore the scriptures, and discover the treasures of wholeness. The apostle Paul tells us in I Thessalonians 5:23; *"And the very God of peace sanctify you wholly; and I pray God your whole spirit and soul and body be preserved blameless unto the coming of our Lord Jesus*

Christ." The book of Thessalonians was among the first of Paul's letters. It was written to encourage the church at Thessalonica. However, it still applies to us today. Paul instructs the believers to live lives of holiness and orderliness. He addresses all three parts of a person; spirit, soul and body. We are not only spirit but we have a soul and we live in a physical body. We are created in the image of our heavenly Father – Father, Son and Holy Spirit.

Paul separated who we are because you can be physically in shape, but have no soundness of mind or we can have a sound mind with an education and no room in our lives for God, which makes us spiritually dead. Yet, we can have a sound mind, be spiritually connected to God and tormented with sickness in our physical bodies.

To be whole is to contain all components. The Encarta Dictionary says to be "complete," indulging all parts or aspects, with nothing left out. Whole means, *"undivided, not divided into parts or not regarded as consisting of separate parts. Not damaged or broken, not wounded, or impaired."* The dictionary defines *whole* as healed or restored to health physically or psychologically.

Being whole constitutes a state where something is complete

and has no parts missing. In other words there is – **NOTHING MISSING, AND NOTHING BROKEN!**

God wants you to be whole and spiritually strong, sound and complete in every area of your life.

CHAPTER 2
Knowing God as Father

"And this is life eternal that they might know thee the only true God, and Jesus Christ, whom thou hast sent" (John 17:3).

Our first journey to wholeness begins with seeking and desiring to have a personal relationship with the Father. There is no wholeness apart from Him. It is important to know who God is. You get to know God the same way you will get to know anyone else, through fellowship. To get to know someone, you have to listen to them and hear what they are saying. You have to become familiar with their character traits by spending time with them. The Bible tells us in John 4:24 *"God is a Spirit."* He is omnipresent—everywhere. He exists simultaneously.

We need to develop an intimacy with the Father. You cannot know God or understand Him with your natural intellect. You are a spirit; you have a soul and you live in a body (I Thess. 5:23). You get to know God through your spirit. You will never know God until your spirit comes in contact with His Spirit. Then you will know Him. Proverbs 20:27 says, *"The spirit of man is the candle of the Lord."* God leads us by our spirit. God instructs our spirit, and our spirit informs our mind and our mind informs our body.

Wholeness is a result of being whole in your spirit by having the right connection with His Spirit.

So let me ask you a question. Do you know Him? God knows you! He knew you before you were born. He knew what you were doing before you purchased this book. God knew you when you were out in the world sinning and saying every nasty thing out of your mouth. He knew if you were a drug addict or alcoholic, or sexually abused. He knew the spouse you would marry, and how many children you would have.

God knew who your mother and father would be. He knows every dark secret you may have and every strand of hair on your head. He is omniscience- He is All knowing. He told Jeremiah,

"Before I formed Thee in the belly, I knew thee: and before thou camest forth out of the womb I sanctified thee, and I ordained thee a prophet unto the nations" (Jeremiah 1:5).

God knows you, but do you know Him?

Do you have a desire to have an intimate relationship with God and to know Him as a special friend? Abraham was called the friend of God. Enoch was called the friend of God and he walked with Him. These men developed an intimate relationship with God, and as a result they did great things. They found their identity in Him. The Father is waiting on you to run to Him and get to know Him better. Jesus said in John 17:3, *"and this is life eternal that they might know thee the only true God, and Jesus Christ whom thou hast sent."* This was Jesus prayer that we would know Him. Paul wanted to know Him and He committed His life to it. He said in Philippians 3:10, *"That I may know Him and the power of his resurrection."* Knowing God will determine the depth and greatness of who you are. How deep is your relationship with Him? Do you have a casual relationship or a deep sincere one?

Knowing God is more than knowing His name, God is Lord. If a person asks you, do you know Carolyn? You responded, yes, but then they ask you how does she like her eggs cooked or does she drink coffee? Could you answer those questions? Knowing a person means you are familiar with and have knowledge of personal information. You know some of their strengths and weaknesses, their likes and dislikes. Knowing God is much the same way. You must know His character and ways. To know Him, we must move from a casual relationship of hearing about Him to an intimate love relationship.

We must go to the scriptures and ask the Holy Spirit, our teacher and guide to introduce us to our Creator, our Father and Lord. We have to fellowship with Him in prayer, praise and worship. Knowing the Father is the first step to becoming whole. **There is no wholeness without the Father.**

Let me introduce you to another scripture to help you understand the importance of knowing God. Isaiah 55:8 states, *"For my thoughts are not your thoughts, neither are your ways my ways, saith the LORD. For as the heavens are higher than the earth, so are my ways higher than your ways, and my thoughts than your thoughts."* God is saying that the natural man receives not the things of the Spirit of God. Your natural way of thinking and natural way of acting are different from God's way.

Man's natural inclination is inferior to God's way. As you take thought, your thoughts will not be the same as His thoughts. So when it comes to your actions, if you don't know the mind of God, you cannot employ God's ways.

God's thoughts are so much higher than our thoughts. He does not have a carnal mind. His ways are not like our ways. He does not operate in the flesh. The Bible says, God is a Spirit and they that know Him, must know Him by the Spirit. We must get to know God so He can reveal to us His ways and thoughts. As you learn more about Him, you will find that He is your father, friend, protector, healer, peace, joy and the all-sufficient One. He is everything you need to live life as a total person.

God's desire is for us to know Him and to know His purpose

and promises for our life. God takes a great deal of pleasure when His children endeavor to know Him. He gets excited when you come to a place of seeking His presence and knowing that you can confidently depend upon Him. Many Christians only know or feel the presence of God at church. Oftentimes, they don't meet Him there. While not the aim, many even allow good intentions, i.e. religious programs and other good things to encroach on God's position in their lives. Webster dictionary defines encroaching as *"to enter by gradual steps or by stealth into the* possessions *or rights of another: to advance beyond the usual or proper limits."* Webster says stealth is *"the act or action of proceeding furtively, secretly or imperceptibly."* In other words, things cross over into our lives through good intentions that are sometimes evil and deceptive. You see, even your good intentions can allow Satan to craftily steer you off course and squeeze the presence of God out. So you must learn how to seek Him each day. You must embrace Him and be resolute about His purpose and position in your life. Glory!

God's constant presence should be the most practical part of your life. You must protect His right in your life. The more time we spend with Him, the better you'll get to know Him. Wholeness requires that we give God the right position in our lives, first! The bible tells us in Matthew 6: 33 to *"seek ye first the kingdom of God, and his righteousness; and all these things shall be added unto you."* For the woman that's whole, a love relationship with God is more important than any other single factor in her life. No other relationship can compare with it.

Do you want God the God you serve to be pleased and excited about you? If you want Him to get excited about you, show Him that you desire to know Him and love Him. You may ask the question, *how do I do that?* Well, this is accomplished by studying and meditating on His Word, through praise and worship, and spending time in prayer. The Bible says, *"If from thence thou shalt seek the LORD thy God, thou shalt find him, if thou seek him with all thy heart and with all thy soul"* (Deuteronomy 4:29). The greatest joy in the world is found in the presence of God. **The fullness of joy is in His presence!**

Wholeness requires that we endeavor to know and understanding the ways of God. Jesus told the disciples, "*It is given to you to know the mysteries of the Kingdom of heaven*" (Matthew 13: 11). When He gathered the disciples around, He told them that He had a story to tell them. The parable started with Him saying, "*the Kingdom of God is as this*," in other words, this is how the Kingdom of God works. He related to them the ways of God. Jesus was not trying to establish another religion or form another set of rules and regulations. He wanted them to know about God and His Kingdom. "*Whereof I am made a minister, according to the dispensation of God which is given to me for you, to fulfill the word of God; Even the mystery which hath been hid from ages and from generations, but now is made manifest to his saints*" (Colossians 1: 25-26). These scriptures indicate that the mysteries were hidden throughout the ages, but are now being revealed through Jesus.

When the disciples returned from their mission they were rejoicing that the demons were subject to them. Jesus told them not to glory because of that, but because their names were written in the Lamb's Book of Life. He also told them that prophets and kings desired to know the things they knew. They wanted to look into that of which you have an opportunity to look into. Jesus warned them that the mysteries had to be given to the right person because everyone would not receive them. Unless you have a true desire to know Him you will not value the revelation that has been made manifest to you as a child of God.

To know God requires belief, trust and obedience.

The children of Israel were without water. They gathered themselves together against Moses and Aaron. Moses and Aaron went to God with the problem. God spoke to Moses and gave him specific instructions. Did he believe, trust and obey? Let's read what happened in Numbers chapter twenty and verses six through twelve. *"And Moses and Aaron went from the presence of the assembly unto the door of the tabernacle of the congregation, and they fell upon their faces: and the glory of the LORD appeared unto them. And the LORD spake unto Moses, saying, Take the rod, and gather thou the assembly together, thou, and Aaron thy brother, and speak ye unto the rock before their eyes; and it shall give forth his water, and thou shalt bring forth to them water out of the rock: so thou shalt give the congregation and their beasts drink. And Moses took the rod from before the LORD, as he commanded him. And Moses and Aaron gathered the congregation together before the rock, and he said unto them, Hear now, ye rebels; must we fetch you water out of this rock? And Moses lifted up his hand, and with his rod he smote the rock twice: and the water came out abundantly, and the congregation drank, and their beasts also. And the LORD spake unto Moses and Aaron, Because ye believed me not."*

Believe Him

God said to Moses that he did not believe Him, and because he did not believe Him, he did not obey Him. When we believe God, we will trust and obey His Word. Moses was angry with the people, and that anger caused disobedience which is a form of unbelief. God was angry with Moses, because Moses, His servant did not believe Him. To know God, you must believe what He says is true and also believe He is sovereign.

Trust Him

Why Moses did not trust God? After all the miracles he saw God perform before his very eyes, he still did not trust him. I believe Moses leaned to his own understanding and his own ways. He forgot that God was in charge of what He had commanded him to do in the first place. When God tells us to do something, we have to trust that He has it all worked out. King Solomon gave us a word of wisdom when he said, "Trust in the LORD with all thine heart; and lean not unto thine own understanding" (Proverbs 3:5). Once again, anger can cause us to distrust. Remember, when God has called you to do something, do your part and then stand firm. When you have done all you can do, leave the situation in God's hands and go on about your business. Do your part. Follow the instructions given to you. It is God who makes us steadfast and establishes us in Christ.

Be Obedient to Him

You must be faithful and obedient to His instructions. Jesus said, *"And why call ye Me, Lord, Lord, and do not the things which I say?" (Luke 6:46).* When you really know Him, there is a desire to be obedient to His every command. It is of utmost importance to know God if you are going to be whole in every area of your life. It starts with Him. Everyone that claims to know God will not enter the kingdom of heaven. In Matthew 7: 21-23, the Bible gives this account of Jesus speaking, *"Not everyone that saith unto me, Lord, Lord, shall enter into the kingdom of heaven; but he that doeth the will of my Father which is in heaven. Many will say to me in that day, Lord, Lord, have we not prophesied in thy name? And in thy name have cast out devils? And in thy name done many wonderful works? And then will I profess unto them, I never knew you: depart from me, ye that work iniquity."*

Many will do the works but will fail to develop a personal relationship with the Father. There are many Christians who will go to church every Sunday. However, they will not pray and fellowship with God. I'm reminded of a movie called *"Left Behind,"* based on the Book of Revelation and scripture in Matthew 13:49. In this movie, Pastors were talking about the great day of the Lord when angels shall come forth, and sever the wicked from the just. Then one day millions of persons left the earth, without notice. The news anchor and authorities questioned one of the pastors because part of his congregation had disappeared. They asked the question, "Why are you still here if what you are telling us that happened is based on the Bible and the beliefs of believers? He responded, "I was so busy teaching others, I never got to know Him personally myself; (paraphrased).

Don't be like this pastor. Endeavor to know Christ so that you can live a life of wholeness on earth and be prepared for life hereafter. I'm talking about a journey to becoming whole.

It starts with knowing the Father and having a personal intimate relationship with Him. When we are whole we obey the voice of God.

Proverbs 20:27 says, *"The spirit of man is the candle of the Lord…"* Romans 8:14 says, *"For as many as are led by the Spirit of God, they are the sons of God."* The Father leads us by our spirit, not our mind or our body. God informs our spirit, and our spirit informs our mind, and our mind leads our body. If you are going to be whole and fulfill your divine destiny, you have to learn to be led by the voice of God. We have to be careful about doing things because we want to do them and saying God told us to do it. Unless you know down in your "knower" (your spirit) that God told you to do something or say something, don't! Do not lie on God! Then there are times when people say, "The devil made me do that." The devil does not make you do anything; you did it because you wanted to do it or because you don't know the ways of God.

You have a will of your own. God will not overpower your will. When we become whole, we then willingly submit our will to His will. Our life becomes His life. It is no longer you that live, but Christ that lives in you.

When you are whole, your number one aim in life is to please God, even when it means going against what you want. When God speaks, learn to follow His voice. Victory in life is won first when we hear and follow the leading of His Spirit.

Hearing God

The Bible tells us in John 10:27, *"My sheep hear my voice."* If you are a born-again child of God, you can hear God speaking to you and you should expect to hear Him. To say you cannot hear His voice is to doubt Him. If I were to ask you if you are one of God's children, no doubt you would probably answer with a "yes!" What if I asked you how do you know, what would you say? You would probably give me Romans 10:9 or else you would say, "I just know!" I know in my spirit! What you are saying is I have a witness in my spirit that bears witness with the Holy Spirit. That inward witness or prompting of the Spirit lets you know that you are saved. It is the same way when God is speaking to us about other things. You will have a prompting in your spirit, or an inner voice speaking to you.

You might be going about your day washing clothes or feeding the children and suddenly you'll think *I need to call my brother.* You may ignore or dismiss the thought at first because you are busy feeding the children, but then the thought occur again. *I need to call my brother.* So you pick up the phone and call your brother, only to find out that He was ill or very depressed. Your call was just in time to pray for him and help during this time of difficulty. This has happened on more than one occasion with me. The Holy Spirit leads us into intercession.

I believe a part of being whole is hearing and being led by the Spirit of God. Wholeness is having our spirit man in tune to Him. If you will learn to live a life listening for that inner witness, expecting to be prompted by the Spirit of God, you will find yourself living each day more and more in agreement and in sync with the Holy Spirit.

When I was living in Texas, some years ago I was prompted by the Holy Spirit to pray, for someone. I thought it was strange that I was moved to pray in the middle of my busy day. I walked out of the door, went to get in the car when the prompting came again. I turned and went back into the house, kneeled and started praying. I knew something wasn't right. I knew something was wrong. My prayer was intense!

A few hours later, I received a phone call that the person I was praying for had been in a terrible car accident. I asked the caller when and what time did it happen. It was the exact time that the prompting of the Spirit led me to pray for them. The police said, "This was a miracle that she did not die instantly." WOW, that's why knowing God and staying in fellowship with Him is so important. **Fellowship is one of the keys to wholeness!** Listening to the voice of God and following His promptings can save a life! That life might be yours.

A Heavenly Viewpoint

Knowing God is having a heavenly viewpoint. I love beautiful things and have been blessed with many. But, things don't have me. The world would like for us to think that we are less than whole if we don't possess a lot of stuff. Some even relate wholeness as having prosperity to their possessions. However, this is far from the truth. Wholeness is much more than things. Wholeness comes first through an intimate relationship with the Father. Secondly, wholeness is developed as we believe, trust and obey Him. And thirdly, wholeness comes from having the right perspective about our spirit man and eternity.

Over and over in the scriptures, we see a contrast of poorly spent lives verses wisely spent lives. Jesus told us not to spend our lives storing up treasures on earth where they are subject to destruction, but to lay up treasures in heaven where they would never be destroyed. If all your treasure is on earth you will have very little interest in heaven. **No interest in heaven, no wholeness**!

The Bible tells us to *"Lay not up for yourselves treasures upon earth, where moth and rust doth corrupt, and where thieves break through and steal: But lay up for yourselves treasures in heaven, where neither moth nor rust doth corrupt, and where thieves do not break through nor steal: For where your treasure is, there will your heart be also"* (Matthew 6:19-21). What we do with our time is important. So are you wasting your time trying to accomplish things on earth which are fruitless pursuits, or are you building treasures in heaven? A person who has become whole is heavenly minded. They realize that we have only one life and only what we do for Christ will last.

There is only one way to transfer anything from earth to heaven and that is what we do for the glory of God. *"Whether therefore ye eat, or drink, or whatsoever ye do, do all to the glory of God"* (I Corinthians 10:31). No one ever has, or ever will take any of the world's goods with them into eternity. Lives and lifetimes have been spent gaining more and more, many times with more and more sorrow. With this one life you have been given, desire to live it in wholeness in Christ.

When I think about my life I realize that my treasure is in *heaven, where neither moth nor rust doth corrupt, and where thieves do not break through nor steal: For where your treasure is, there will your heart be also"* (Matthew 6:19-21). My heart is in God!

I have a BIG imagination! Time is not long enough to fulfill all the visions and dreams that my mind can imagine. If Michael Jackson was still alive, he would tell you that he had one more song that he wanted to sing. If Rembrandt was living, he would have one more picture he wanted to paint. If Einstein was alive, he would have one more invention. Smith Wigglesworth would have one more sermon. The apostle Paul said that *"If in this life only we have hope in Christ, we are of all men most miserable" (I Corinthians 15:19)*. God wants us to live in fullness and wholeness!

Wholeness is a life rich toward God!

CHAPTER 3
Wholesome Thinking

*"And be not conformed to this world: but be ye transformed by
the renewing of your mind, that ye may prove what is that good,
and acceptable, and perfect, will of God" (Romans 12:2).*

The mind is one of God's greatest creations. The human brain is probably the most complex arrangement of matter in the universe. We have an incredible machine inside our head called a "brain." I like to refer to it as a physical computer, storing files of information. Inside the skull of your head is more information stored than in your local library. Your brain is incredible, and it only weighs about three pounds.

Psychologists tell us that each person has about ten thousand thoughts per day. WOW! Did you realize that so many thoughts go through your mind each day? Unbelievable! It means that we have many chances of having good and bad thoughts each day.

The human thought process remains a mystery to scientists and psychologists. However, one thing is sure about the mind, how you think will direct your life and affect your walk with God.

God has given you the ability to do great things – through the power of the mind. So before you can move from where you are to where you want to be, you have to **first move** in your mind.

Before you can accomplish great things you have to first see what you want to accomplish in your mind. I call it the "mind's eye." The Bible tells us in Proverbs 23:7a *"For as he thinketh in his heart, so is he."*

The Great King Solomon tells us that we are as we think. Therefore, if you want to change your life you have to change your thinking! If you want to increase your life – you have to be willing to increase your thinking. Your mind has the ability to change your relationships – your career – your finances – your health – your environment – and your appearance by the way you think. Your life is a set of thoughts demonstrated over a period of time.

To be whole you have to change the process of your <u>thinking</u> from the old way of thinking to the kingdom way of thinking!

We have two options for how we live our life: with Jesus Christ or without Him. We cannot live a life that's pleasing to God and at the same time please the world. When you and I come to a saving knowledge of Jesus Christ, we are given a new beginning and a fresh start. We are forgiven for our past and given wisdom for handling life. The apostle Paul tells us *"If anyone is in Christ, he is a new creation; old things have passed away, behold, all things have become new" (2 Corinthians 5:17).* In addition to being our Savior, Jesus is our model for how to live.

The Bible says that *"Jesus increased in wisdom"* (Luke 2:52). Jesus grew and He increased in the things of God. We should purposefully seek the knowledge of God to become more like Him. To be like Him, our minds must be renewed to the laws of God.

To gain knowledge as to why our minds have to be renewed, let's go to the Bible and look at scriptures. When Adam disobeyed God, his spirit man died. His soulish man (his mind) and his carnal man connected together to rule His life. The carnal man had the greater power or strength. Through Adam's sin, evil entered the life of each of us. God said to Cain in Genesis 4: 6-7 *"Why art thou wroth? and why is thy countenance fallen? If thou doest well, shalt thou not be accepted? If thou doest not well, sin lieth at the door. And unto thee shall be his desire, and thou shalt rule over him."*

It makes no difference when we were saved; sin isn't far away from our door! Sin is with us as long as we live in this world. So how do we live a holy life? How do we keep the sin nature from ruling in our lives? Let's go to the scriptures and see what apostle Paul tells us in Romans 8: 5- 7. *"For they that are after the flesh, do mind the things of the flesh; but they that are after the Spirit the things of the Spirit. For to be carnally minded is death; but to be spiritually minded is life and peace. Because the carnal mind is enmity against God: for it is not subject to the law of God, neither indeed can be."*

The Mind of the Flesh

The mind of the flesh which is the carnal mind with its thoughts and purposes is hostile to God. It does not submit itself to God's ways or laws. Paul said, indeed, it cannot! When we are saved, our spirit man is born again, but our minds have to be renewed to the ways of the Kingdom. I believe we can be saved and for a season still have the carnal nature. I see it all the time. New coverts come into the body of Christ, and the worldly ways are still there. And unless, the right teaching takes place that person will struggle with Christianity because their carnal nature make them question their salvation. They don't fully understand how they can accept Jesus as their Savior, and still have some of the same old habits and behaviors. In the great Exodus, Moses led the Israelites out of Egypt. They were no sooner across the Red Sea before many of them began to long for the "leeks and garlic" of Egypt. They were happy to be from Egyptian bondage, but they had not let go of all they had known during their time of slavery. They had come out of Egypt, but all of Egypt had not come out of them.

I remember a saying that I heard while I was working in the

cotton fields. It went like this, *"You can take a person out of the country but you can't take the country out of them."* I had no idea what that meant, but now I understand what it means. You can go from one location to another, but the same behavior will occur unless your mind has changed. A transformation of the mind has to take place for a change of behavior to take place. If you only change the environment then things won't really change. A change has to take place in the soul realm. Where the mind goes, you will follow; as a matter of fact the mind usually gets there first.

Is your life being transformed by the Word of God? What are you feeding into your mind? Are you heeding the biblical truths and warnings about the danger of "garbage in, garbage out?" We have to guard our minds from things that will contribute to an unhealthy and unholy lifestyle.

You have to decide what you are going to feed your mind. Are you watching the negative, evil movies that glorify the devil, or are you watching wholesome movies that will not feed evil into your spirit? We cannot listen to wrong music and watch pornography and think that it will not affect our thought process. **Remember "garbage in, garbage out."**

I heard Dr. Creflo A. Dollar Jr., pastor of World Changers Church International say in a message he was preaching, "Watch your thoughts for they become words, watch your words for they become actions, watch your actions for they become habits, watch your habits for they become character, watch your character for it becomes your destiny." WOW! Destiny begins with a thought!

The struggle is always there between our carnal or natural man and the spirit man. Paul writes about the struggle he has in Romans 7: 14-23. *"For we know that the law is spiritual: but I am carnal, sold under sin. For that which I do I allow not: for what I would, that do I not; but what I hate, that do I. If then I do that which I would not, I consent unto the law that it is good. Now then it is no more I that do it, but sin that dwelleth in me. For I know that in me (that is, in my flesh,) dwelleth no good thing: for to will is present with me; but how to perform that which is good I find not. For the good that I would I do not: but the evil which I would not, that I do. Now if I do that I would not, it is no more I that do it, but sin that dwelleth in me. I find then a law, that, when I would do good, evil is present with me. For I delight in the law of God after the inward man: But I see another law in my members, warring against the law of my mind, and bringing me into captivity to the law of sin which is in my members."*

Paul said it is no longer I who do what I do, but sin principle which is at home in me, and has possession of me. Then he goes on to say, if I do what I don't desire to do, it is not myself acting, but the sin principle which is fixed and operates in my soul. He says that the sin principle, which is the ability or desire to sin, is fixed and operating in his soul. Paul had to beat his flesh daily and make his mind and flesh obey the ways of the spirit.

Becoming Whole in our Minds

Mind renewal is the key to living a successful life as a Christian and overcoming the mindset that keep us bound in ungodly lifestyles. It is the key that will open the door to the blessings. Jesus said, *"I am come that they might have life, and that they might have it more abundantly"* (John 10:10b). He wants us to prosper in every area of our life. It starts with the way you think. You cannot do what you cannot think to do and you cannot go where you cannot think. Some of us are living at a level lower than God intended because our thought process has held us to a certain place in life.

When we change our thought process and remove the wrong thinking, our spirit man will be free to create and to produce fruit in our lives. My mother use to tell me and my siblings, "that you cannot be what you cannot think." She said, **"Think BIG!"** God does not want you sitting on the sideline watching others become blessed and fulfilling their dreams and living a life of abundance. You were not created to be a spectator in life. You were created to have the mind of Christ. Thanks mom!

The Word of God will renew your mind.

God's Word will help you to conquer whatever is holding or preventing you from living out your purpose to the fullest.

The Bible says in James 1:*21 "Wherefore lay apart all filthiness and superfluity of naughtiness, and receive with meekness the engrafted word, which is able to save your souls (mind)."* James is referring to the moral impurity and the evil to which moral impurity will lead. These things can be laid aside only by your understanding that all things come through Christ Jesus and what He did at the cross. He said lay all evil aside and then receive the Word and it will save your soul.

The apostle Paul reminds us to not be conformed any longer to the pattern of this world, but be transformed by the renewing of your mind. When you become born again your spirit instantly changes; you are recreated in Christ Jesus (2 Corinthians 5:17). Yet, your mind is not recreated! It must be renewed. We didn't get a perfectly renewed mind that only thinks the things of God and confessed His promises routinely. We didn't instantly stop thinking evil thoughts; stop murmuring and complaining. We didn't instantly stop listening to the old-man nature and start listening to God. God has given us the tool to renew our minds, His Word! To manifest the power of God in our lives we must renew it to the Word of God.

When I first received salvation, I loved those mini-skirts. It didn't change instantly, I still wore them. I was saved, but my mouth was not saved. I still spoke some profane language. I loved to go out dancing, partying and having "spirits," to make me feel good. (It wasn't the Holy Spirit). As I studied more of the Word, my mind was transformed and those old ways of the natural man ceased in allowing me to live a more purified life, a better wholesome life.

The Word *"renewing"* is the Greek word *metamorphoo* which is to be transformed or trans-figured in the same manner the caterpillar changes into a butterfly. We must also be transformed so that we will stop being conformed to this world and its evil influences and allow our minds to become a habitat of God's Word. To renew is to make new or to restore to its original state. We must renew our thinking continually and on purpose. It is not an overnight, one-time event.

How do we transform the mind? Paul said, *"But put ye on the Lord Jesus Christ, and make not provision for the flesh, to fulfill the lusts thereof"* (Romans 13:14). How are you going to put on the Lord Jesus Christ? In your mind! Paul was a living example of someone walking with God. He was always about His Father's business; studying His Word and speaking it to others.

Renewing the mind takes a conscious effort on our part to stop thinking the negative, unbelieving thoughts of the world (the habit of our old man) and put into our minds the exceeding great and precious promises of God.

The new man that is spiritually-minded appears when we take an active part in renewing our minds to the Word of God. Through reading the Scriptures and meditating on them, your thinking will be transformed and you'll have the mind of Christ, *"To prove what is that good and acceptable and perfect will of God."*

To renew your mind to God's Word is essential.

Apostle Paul said in First Corinthians 2:16 *"For who hath known the mind of the Lord, that he may instruct him? But we have the mind of Christ."* No one has known the mind of God. He instructs, because He knows all; therefore, none can instruct Him. But those who have the mind of Christ see things as God sees them. They will think His thoughts. The Bible instructs us to *"Let this mind be in you, which was also in Christ Jesus"* (Philippians 2:5).

The Power of Wholesome Thinking!

God wants you recognize the power within you and the

awesomeness of your mind. **Your mind is an incredible creation!** It holds tremendous creative ability. God gave you an imagination – so that you can create mental pictures and bring forth that which you create in your thoughts. Once you have an image in your mind of what you want to do or become, all you have to do is ADD FAITH to your works, and the mental image of the desired object will manifest in your life.

King Solomon instructs us in Proverbs 23: 12 to *"Apply thine heart unto instruction, and thine ears to the words of knowledge."* We need to know something if we are going to be successful in this life. What you don't know can hurt you. We have to take time to put something healthy into our minds. Although, there is a wealth of knowledge in the Bible, there are also many great books, journals, and writings by anointed women and men who have been inspired by God. This information is available to help us to develop a wholesome mind. SO READ AND APPLY THE SCRIPTURES!

Time to Meditate

When was the last time you took time to think about what you were thinking about? Have you ever stopped to listen to yourself talk? Have you evaluated the results by your thinking or the lack of your thinking? What are you daily meditating on? STOP! Take the time to work on your mind! You may be just one thought away from greatness! Whatever you meditate on will become the blueprint for your reality.

God told Joshua, *"This book of the law shall not depart out of thy mouth; but thou shalt meditate therein day and night, that thou mayest observe to do according to all that is written therein: for then thou shalt make thy way prosperous, and then thou shalt have good success"* (Joshua 1:8). So heed what it says, meditate, obey the Word, and you will prosper and have good success!

CHAPTER 4
He Wants It All

"For ye are bought with a price: therefore glorify God in your body, and in your spirit, which are God's" (1 Corinthians 6:20).

What does the body have to do with being a "Total Woman"? Everything! God wants it all! Yes, He wants your spirit, soul and body to be whole. He said to glorify Me in your body. We should not just be beautiful on the outside but inside as well. God created beauty! He wants us to be beautiful ladies, and we are! It is Godly beauty that glorifies Him. The world's definition and God's definition of beauty is different. Let's explore the difference.

The world presses us to achieve the "ideal" image of beauty. Over the last centuries, dozens of television programs are designed to turn Cinderella into the princess. Many weight lost commercials are geared toward helping individuals reduce their size. I watched the television show "Extreme Makeover" where ladies were given facial and fashion makeovers along with fashion advice. They were chosen for their lives to be changed through a one time physical makeover. I think this was good to help boost their self-esteem. But the only lasting makeover starts from the inside.

The field of cosmetic surgery continues to grow as the demand for non-surgical procedures increase. Face lifts, abdominoplasty, breast augmentations and reductions, eyelid surgery, lipoplasty, botox, and permanent make-up…WOW! If you need or desire it, you can purchase it. If you don't like it, you can change it. I believe every woman has looked in the mirror and has seen something she would like to change about her outer appearance. I know I have.

Whether it is your eyes, the wrinkles over the forehead, thin lips, or the big nose… Some of us have looked in the mirror and wanted to decrease our hips, enlarge our breast, take away or add something. We believe we would feel much better if we could just change what we don't like about ourselves.

Every woman in the United States is part of a daily beauty pageant, whether she likes it or not. Why? The reason is that we are surrounded by a popular culture that is saturated with images of idealized and unattainable female physical beauty. We cannot escape the feeling that we are judged on the basis of our outer appearance. Many women feel insecure and have low self-esteem as thin beauty images parade before them in magazines, on television and billboards. The cosmetic and fashion industries exploit thin beautiful ladies as the standard of beauty for all women. This applies pressure to women on all levels to maintain a certain level of appearance. Even young girls go to the extreme to be beautiful!

To achieve beauty is a desire in the lives of most women regardless of age. If you search the internet for "beauty secrets," over 40 million web pages will pop up. Women in the United States are spending an enormous amount of money on cosmetic products. That's not to mention the hair industry. WOW! What a business? Reports show that almost a total of $7 billion is spent per year on cosmetics alone.

Money spent on cosmetic surgery and non-surgical aesthetic procedures is increasing drastically among women. Based on the increase in the cosmetic industry, surgical and non-surgical cosmetic procedures to the outer appearance of a woman are extremely, important, and it should be. With all the money we spend each year, and all the trouble that we go through to look beautiful, does it work by itself? I think not.

We focus on the outer appearance hoping to meet the world's standards. Your inner beauty is not something that others can manufacture or mix with a chemical or a dye. Inner beauty cannot be created no matter what we buy.

Inner beauty is a gift from God.

I went to modeling school and spent several years as a fashion model. I loved it! I loved wearing new clothes and walking down the run way. Fashion shows, market buying, cosmetics, jewelry and clothes were my thing. I loved it so much that I was blessed to open my own boutique in a mall outside of Dallas, Texas. I wore a new outfit every day. Was I fulfilled? No! I was missing something. The outer appearance was not enough to fulfill the inner woman. What is going on in the inside will reflect on the outside. If you don't feel beautiful, you won't appear confident. When you don't like who you are, it will show on the outside.

When you have low self-esteem, it will be noticeable. Sin will rob you of your self-esteem and cause you to feel ugly regardless of how beautiful you look on the outside. Guilt and shame will eat away at you like a parasite and make you feel unattractive. Dresses and fine jewelry cannot hide the inner man. Many ladies try to cover up their pain, past and guilt with their make-up, clothes and hair. I did, but I discovered that the best make-over is the makeover of the spirit and not the makeup of the flesh. You can wear the finest fashions and the most expensive jewelry and look good on the outside, but still be broken.

How I was Made Over

I began my spiritual makeover, by first silencing my inner critic. That voice on the inside that judged me for past mistakes and made me feel worthless, had to go. I replaced it with what God said about me. I reprogrammed my inner voice. I forgave myself of past mistakes and made a decision to move on. *Secondly,* I took my eyes off of others and looked to myself. I found there were hidden treasures within that needed to be developed. God gave me self-worth, and I needed to feel good about me. *Thirdly,* I got rid of all the teachings and false beliefs I received from others that were negative programming. Those files were erased and replaced with *"I can do all things through Christ who strengthens me." Next,* I changed my circle of friends. My mother use to say, *"If you tell me who you run with, I will tell you who you are."* I never forgot that. Once again, thanks mom. I begin to socialize with people with good self-esteem, who set goals for their lives and were not jealous or envious of my success. The people you hang around with can either add to your self-esteem or take away from it. You need a support system of friends and family who are accommodating of the person you are and are becoming. Good friends are a double gift – one you benefit from, and the other person benefits from as well.

The *fifth* thing I did was feed my mind and spirit with positive Words from the Bible. Peter told us, to *"... add to my faith goodness; and to goodness, knowledge; and to knowledge, self-control; and to self-control, perseverance; and to perseverance, godliness; and to godliness, mutual affection; and to mutual affection, love"* (2 Peter 1:5-7). The perfect accessory is love, and the right color is joy. Through the study of the Word, I was able to clothe myself in kindness, humility, gentleness, and patience. I found true beauty within, then boldness, self-assurance, self-confidence and God-confidence came.

Lastly, I gave myself permission to be me. There is no one else exactly like me, or you. **God's creations are unique.** No one else here on this earth can to do what God has called me to do, or what He has called you to do.

Being free to be you, adds beauty to your life. I affirmed myself! Other's approval is important, but if having the approval of others means giving up yourself, you don't have to have it. I've learned to celebrate the uniqueness of God's creation. You should too!

God said to Samuel, *"For the Lord does not see as man see; for man looks at the outward appearance, but the Lord looks at the heart"*(1 Samuel 16:7). God's desire is for us to be beautiful from the inside out. Things might appear beautiful on the outside, but if we are not together on the in-side, it will show in our attitudes and the way we approach life.

One of my favorite Bible stories is the Samaritan woman who met Jesus at the well. She came to the well in the heat of the day when no one else would be there. Her shame and pain of the past made her feel ugly and unworthy. Jesus gave her a makeover and removed the mask she had been wearing. It was not a physical makeover, but a spiritual makeover.

He confronted her problems and caused her to look within herself. And Jesus said unto her, *"Go, call thy husband, and come hither. The woman answered and said, I have no husband. Jesus said unto her, Thou hast well said, I have no husband: For thou hast had five husbands; and he whom thou now hast is not thy husband: in that saidst thou truly"* (John 4:16-18).

You cannot conquer that which you do not Face and acknowledge. The woman at the well faced her problems and it opened the door for God to do a makeover on her that day. No longer did she have to carry the burden of low self esteem and feelings of guilt. She was set free! As a female and from the knowledge of many years of counseling women, I can imagine that her countenance and her smile changed. She probably changed her style of clothing. Her body language was now one of confidence and pride. She felt good on the inside and now it radiated on the outside!

When she went back to the city, she told others about meeting Jesus. They heard her but they also saw that something was different. Her inner perception of herself changed her outer appearance.

Remember your inner feelings will reflect to the outside. Spiritual makeover has to start from within!

Peter reminds us *"Whose adorning let it not be that outward adorning of plaiting the hair, and of wearing of gold, or of putting on of apparel; "But let it be the hidden man of the heart, in that which is not corruptible, even the ornament of a meek and quiet spirit, which is in the sight of God of great price"* (1 Peter 3:3-4). Ladies, there's nothing wrong with looking good. I advocate that, but real beauty is within and out.

One day I was shopping at a major department store in the shoe department, (I love shoes). As I was admiring the new styles and colors, a young lady walked in who immediately got my attention. She was beautiful. Everything was in place: the hair, shoes, purse, nail polish, and outfit. Her appearance was well put together with everything matching. I thought to myself she is really awesome and has it all together. It was a little busy in the store so she had to wait a few minutes. Finally, the sales associate asked if she could help her. When she opened her mouth I could not believe what I was hearing. The words that came out of her mouth did not match what I saw at all. It was quite embarrassing. The Bible says, *"out of the abundance of the heart the mouth speaks"* (Matthew 12:34).

Do not let your appearance become more important than your character? It is crucial to avoid sending the wrong messages. Your outer appearance is important – but the beauty inside is more important! **God wants you to be beautiful inside and outside.** He created you to be beautiful. You were fearfully and wonderfully made! When I think about that, it sounds beautiful.

The most important characteristic is how you feel about you. Your self-esteem will reflect how you act, how you relate to others, and what you achieve. You have been given the freedom to feel good about yourself. So go ahead; God will approve. He will respond to us when we give Him our heart and soul. Like the facets of a diamond, each detail of an individual adds something to the WHOLE.

YOUR BODY-Is Important?

"I beseech you therefore, brethren, by the mercies of God, that ye present your bodies a living sacrifice, holy, acceptable unto God, which is your reasonable service: (Romans 12:1). Paul said that we are to "present *our* bodies *as a living sacrifice, holy, acceptable to God, which is our spiritual worship."* He wants not only our spirits and mind, but our bodies. Your body counts; it matters to God. You belong to God, spirit, soul and body, and He wants it all!

I know you are probably thinking why would God be interested in my body? It's old, thin, over or underweight, wrinkled, cellulite, diseased, unattractive, awkward, near-sighted, has a stigmatism, arthritis and hard-of-hearing. You may be anxious, impatient, stressed, tired and overloaded. What kind of sacrifice is that? God is not asking for a sacrifice for sin. Jesus Christ took care of that on the cross. That is why a body like ours is acceptable to Him. 1 Peter 2:5 tells us *"Ye also, as lively stones, are built up a spiritual house, an holy priesthood, to offer up spiritual sacrifices, acceptable to God by Jesus Christ."* Peter tells us the same as Paul did in Romans chapter twelve and verse one to *"offer spiritual sacrifices acceptable to God"*—then Peter adds these words: *"through Jesus Christ."* We're acceptable to God because of Jesus' sacrifice.

The offering of our bodies is not the offering of our physical looks but our **bodily behavior**. In the Bible, God makes it clear that the body is not significant because of the way it looks, but because of the way it acts (1 Samuel 16:7). Our body is given to us to make visible the beauty of Christ. The beauty of Christ is the beauty of love, and not the beauty of looks. His beauty was the beauty of sacrifice for all mankind.

God does not demand our bodies because he wants super models. He demands our bodies because he wants models of kindness, love and mercy. God wants visible bodily evidence that our lives are built on his love. *"Presenting a living holy body to God"* means giving Him our members— our eyes, our tongue, our ears, our hands and our feet. It means giving our body to righteousness, not sin. That is what makes a body holy! A body is holy not because of what it looks like, but because of what it does. Hallelujah!

The writer of Hebrews 13:16 says, *"Do not neglect to do good and to share what you have, for such sacrifices are pleasing to God."* When you do good works, in Jesus' name, with the members of your body, it becomes a holy, living sacrifice of worship, and it is pleasing to God!

Is your body a physical instrument of compassion and peace? Is it an instrument of righteousness and joy? Is it a physical instrument that walks in the fruit of the spirit, or is it a body that is just adorned with beautiful clothes, make-up and jewelry? Is it a body that looks great on *the* outside, but does not glorify our Heavenly Father? Think on these questions and endeavor to honor God in your body. Show the worth of Christ and His holiness by the way you present and use your body. Amen.

Our Body - THE TEMPLE

"What? know ye not that your body is the temple of the Holy Ghost which is in you, which ye have of God, and ye are not your own?" *(1 Corinthians 6:19)* God loves your physical body and it is very precious to Him. Jesus showed God's love for our bodies when He healed people. Throughout the gospels, we see Jesus going about healing all that were sick and oppressed by the devil. Why? He wanted the body to be WHOLE. God dwells in our physical bodies and calls the body His temple. Think about it. Our bodies are temples; sacred sites where God dwells. People should be able to come to us as temples of the living God, and meet Him there!

God has a plan and purpose for your life and that plan involves your physical body. It began when you were in your mother's womb. God made us, and He knows us. He saw us as we were forming in the womb. God knew your body as it was developing in the womb!

There are no unimportant people. You are not insignificant. God did not make you to be defective, but to be effective. Do not betray yourself. He does not make any copy cats or junk!

King David knew that he was the work of God's hands. He looked on his body with the eyes of faith and said in Psalm 139:14 *"I will praise thee; for I am fearfully and wonderfully made: marvellous are thy works; and that my soul knoweth right well."* I love this scripture. I often look on my little frame and rejoice even though I would have desired to have thicker hair. Yet, marvelous are His works! As I stated in the first chapter, God took time and shaped the woman. My soul is happy. I enjoy being a woman! His creation is marvelous. We have to take care of what God has carefully created so it will bring Him the glory it deserves. *"So let the beauty of the Lord our God be upon us"* (Psalm 90:17). Hallelujah!

Discipline the Body

The longer I serve the Lord, the more I realize the desperate need for discipline. Apostle Paul tells us that we are in a race. I want to finish my course strong. Also, I want to have the energy to complete my assignment and look good while I am doing it. Don't you? *"Know ye not that they which run in a race run all, but one receiveth the prize? So run, that ye may obtain. And every man that striveth for the mastery is temperate in all things. Now they do it to obtain a corruptible crown; but we an incorruptible. I therefore so run, not as uncertainly; so fight I, not as one that beateth the air: But I keep under my body, and bring it into subjection: lest that by any means, when I have preached to others, I myself should be a castaway"* (I Corinthians 9: 24-27).

Paul said he had to discipline his body and we have to do the same. My favorite past time next to reading is eating out. I love fine restaurants! I love the atmosphere and ambiance.

When my husband and I travel, we look for great restaurants that are cozy with a great atmosphere and good food. However, we have to watch very carefully of what we eat. So discipline has become a major part of our favorite past time. Let's get real about it. Many of us over eat. We need to have MORE DISCIPLINE WITH OUR EATING HABITS.

Daughters of the King, glorify God with your body! You have heard the saying, "beauty is only skin-deep." Well, that is only partially true. The inner beauty is developed as a result of a relationship with Jesus Christ. The outer beauty is our part. **Beauty is both inside and outside!** After adorning ourselves in the inner man, we have to take care of the physical body. You are a precious diamond, a bejeweled tiara! God made you special! We have to look in the mirror and be truthful with ourselves. Are we overweight? Does our body please God? I want you to think about it. Don't cover up or try to hide the truth. This is a good time to look in the mirror and see what God sees. He's aware of it if you have a struggle with over eating.

Let's look at some facts related to being overweight or obese. Obesity increases the risk of heart disease, Type 2 Diabetes, high blood pressure, stroke, breathing problems, arthritis, gallbladder disease, sleep apnea, osteoarthritis and some cancers. For many women, carrying extra weight around their waists or middle raises health risks such as heart disease and cancer, more than if they carry extra weight around their hips or thighs. If you are overweight or obese, get real and begin to work on it. Do not hide it anymore. "You shall know the truth, and the truth shall make you free…" The book of Proverbs encourages us *to "buy the truth, and sell it not"* (23:23). Buy the truth about yourself and dedicate yourself to the task of losing the weight.

Keep in mind that God loves you, and He will never leave you or forsake you. You can do all things through Christ, but you have to get started. Physical activity is important to weight reduction. OUCH! Physical activity is my area of weakness. But I am working on it. I encourage you to take thirty minutes a day to exercise and begin to eat smaller portions. Get an accountability partner to help you. My husband and I help each other to be accountable for our weight. It works!

Pray this prayer. Lord Jesus, thank you for the inward beauty you have created in me! Help me so that my physical body can reflect your beauty outwardly for all to see you. Amen.

Now believe that God will help and begin a physical weight reduction regiment. You can do it. You have favor. You are a winner and God wants you to be healthy in spirit, soul and body.

Many of the physical manifestations are symptoms of a spiritual or emotional problem. Ask yourself, what is eating me? What hunger am I trying to satisfy with food? Could it be your eating habits were developed to soothe emotional wounds? Look deeply and see if there are some old hurts that need to be healed or some things you need to release. Maybe you need to forgive someone or maybe you need to forgive yourself.

Overeating is not the only way we harm our bodies. Cigarette smoking, excessive alcohol, free-floating, anger and other destructive behaviors harm our bodies also. Allow me to speak about anger. It is a big deterrent to beauty. I have witnessed women, yes Bible toting, God confessing women, with a short fuse. You say the wrong thing and it's like setting off a bomb. They go into orbit. Sister, that's a bad witness for God. Anger can keep you from being whole. The Bible says, *"for anger resteth in the bosom of fools"* (Ecclesiastes 7:9). I know you don't want to be labeled as a fool. Thus, get a hold of yourself and begin to work on your anger issue. It's a part of the process of presenting your body to God as a living sacrifice and becoming whole in every area.

CHAPTER 5
The Woman of Faith

"Daughter, be of good comfort; thy faith hath made thee whole" (Matthew 9:22).

A total woman is a woman of faith. No one can be whole or live a successful life without faith. The Bible **says that without faith, it is impossible to please God (Hebrews 11:6).** Faith is essential to wholeness. It is the currency of heaven, without it you get nothing from God. The total woman chooses daily to walk by faith. She realizes that it is the key to pleasing God. In the lives of all great women, there is one essential ingredient—faith. It is central to living a total life of abundance.

Faith is the key to open the door of success, but it can be the lock on the door that keeps you from success. But just what is faith? Faith is the title deed to things hoped for and the proof that you have them when you believe. Trust, belief and optimism are the attributes of the one who walks by faith and not by sight. But how do you obtain faith? The Bible tells us that, *"Faith cometh by hearing, and hearing by the word of God"* (Romans 10:17).

Faith is birthed in your spirit by hearing what God has said and believing it. We either live by faith, or we live in fear. So we must chose faith over fear. Daily women are faced with situations that require them to exercise their faith: issues centered around their husbands, children, job, finances and health. In each situation, she must choose to believe the promises of God or chose to live in fear.

None of us are immune to fear. But worry, fear, and wrong thinking are not simply bad habits. They are indications of a lack of faith.

Jesus, in Mark eleven and verse twenty-two, told His disciples to have the **God-kind of faith** when He said to them, "…Have faith in God." Every woman that is whole focuses on her faith and let God deal with her fears. When we stay in faith we have great expectations. We expect God's favor to work on our behalf. God cannot ignore faith. Faith is powerful! It moves mountains and without faith you will never live an abundant life.

The Power of Faith

We, as humans, are limited by our senses and our understanding. But, due to the gift of faith, which gives us assurance, we can have the power to overcome our limitations. Faith gives us **power to see the unseen.** When we look through the eyes of faith we can see God. Although God is Spirit, I see Him through His handiwork of creation and his work in my life. Faith gives us the ability to see future things that have been promised to us by God.

When there is no faith in the future there is no power in the present. **Faith gives us the power to hear what can't be heard through the natural ear**. Through faith one can hear the voice of God. You may have never heard God speak in an audible voice, but you can hear Him speak in a still, small voice, through your circumstances, through His Word and through godly counsel.

Faith gives us the **power to comprehend the incomprehensible.** There will be times in our lives when things occur, which absolutely cannot be explained or understood with our human or the rational mind. For example, sometimes terrible things happen to us such as the loss of an opportunity that you worked hard for or the loss of a newborn baby. You might not understand how after wise financial planning, you encountered a financial disaster. These are not easy things to understand, but by faith we can rely upon Romans 8:28, which gives us hope by telling us, *"And we know that all things work together for good to them that love God, to them who are the called according to his purpose."*

Faith gives us **power to do the impossible.** Paul says, in Philippians 3:16 *"I can do all things through Christ which strengtheneth me."* Even when the enemy thinks he has drained every drop of energy from us, faith gives us the ability to stand strong believing in the promises of God. Faith says, I can do it!

Faith gives us the power to believe what is considered to be unbelievable.

A child born to a virgin girl is unbelievable to many. Many stumble over it because only by faith can we believe the Word of God that says Jesus was born of a virgin.

Faith gives us power to attain the unattainable. Man cannot cleanse himself from the penalty of sin. It's by faith we receive salvation. He cannot overcome the reality of death and he cannot live a life pleasing to Christ. Faith gives us the ability to get out of the boat and defy nature to walk on water. It is the power behind the success of a Christian.

Francis Bacon, one of the leading figures in natural philosophy and in the field of scientific methodology during the period of transition from the Renaissance to the early modern era, concluded that a little faith will bring your soul to heaven, but great faith will bring heaven to your soul. So ask yourself: Where is your faith? Whose report do you believe? God's or the enemies report?

There are so many benefits to living by faith. I can't begin to name them all. It's the greatest force in the universe. By faith, God created the world and by faith we create our world. As women, faith is an essential ingredient in our lives to be whole and complete.

Faith-Filled Women

As previously stated, the Bible is filled with examples of women of faith. We will begin with the two women named in Hebrews chapter eleven, which is referred to as the Hall of Faith. Sarah was esteemed with the honor of being in the Hall of Faith because by faith she conceived a child in her old age. She started off rocky and laughed when God told her she would have a child, but she received faith to judge God as faithful to his promise. That's what you must do. Believe that God will honor His Word.

God has not forgotten what He has told you. You may be saying, "God has forgotten. He promised to give me a husband or a child." But, God hasn't forgotten. No matter how long it's been, God still remembers. God says, no, no, no, my daughter I remember! I put the desire in your heart, and I'm going to fulfill it. You may have written off your dream, but God remembers it. So get back in faith. God is going to bring it to past. When God remembers, it doesn't matter how long it takes or how impossible it may look, God will do as He has promised. **Your dream has no expiration date!**

The next woman of faith we will explore is Rahab, the harlot. She is in the Hall of Faith as well. In the book of Joshua, we encounter this woman of faith who made a decision to believe what she had heard about God, and it changed her life. Rabah was a prostitute and like many women today, maybe even some reading this book, she made the wrong decision about the worth of her body. But in Joshua chapter two, it is recorded that she makes the right decision to help the Israelite spies, and it saved her and her entire family. What convinced her to betray her own people to save the lives of people she had never seen before? It was her faith in what she had heard about God.

Woman of God, you develop in faith when you believe what you hear about God. He is your Provider, Protector and Banner of Victory. He is the Great I Am, that means He is who you need Him to be at the time you need Him to be it. He'll be your husband, the father you didn't have, and your banker. But you must believe it and you must act on what you believe. James the Apostle tells us **that faith without works is dead.** Wishing will not make it so. You must do something. If you need more income, look for a better job, go back to school or ask God for a witty invention. Exercise your faith. It is like a muscle; the more you use it, the better it works. If you are saying, "Someday I'm going to get out of debt," it will never happen until you make a plan to get out of debt. Maybe, a good place to start is to stop spending so much for shoes and purses. In other words, put a plan in place and by faith work the plan.

Rahab did something that changed her life. In the end, she was a "total woman." She put her faith to work by helping the spies. She knew enough about God to believe He would care for His own. How about you? Do you believe God will meet all your needs? Rabah's faith earned her a position in the genealogy of our Lord Jesus Christ? How about that as a benefit for believing what you hear about God?

Speaking Faith-Filled Words

Maybe you could start releasing your faith by speaking faith-filled words. You'll have what you say, you know. If you are speaking fear, don't expect to have success. Words have power and the Bible says, *"You eat the fruit thereof."* That means you will have what you say. So if you're saying, "I'm ugly, fat, incompetent and unlovable." Don't be surprised if that's how others treat you. If you are saying "I can't make it, I'm always losing, I'll never be well, or nobody likes me." Well, it will be as you say it is. **When you speak faith, you bless yourself. When you speak doubt and unbelief, you curse yourself.**

Take a lesson from the woman with the issue of blood. You'll find her story in Matthew chapter nine. She said to herself *"If I may but touch His garment I shall be whole"* (Matthew 9:21b). **Jesus said her faith made her whole.** Friend, your faith will make you whole. It was after twelve long years of suffering that her faith caused her to be willing to risk being ridiculed to get to Jesus and touch the hem of His garment. So what are you saying to yourself, about yourself and about your situation?

Testing of Your Faith

How would you like to fly on an airplane that had not yet been tested? Imagine the builders have just finished building the aircraft and said alright, get on it. But nobody has tested the individual parts and nobody tested to see how it was put together. If you can't test it, you can't trust it. How would you like to know that you are going to be the first patient a surgeon operates on? We like the comfort of something that has already been tested. So how do you know that your faith is real unless it stands the test?

Jesus tested the Syro-Phoenician woman's faith. She believed that Jesus would heal her demon-possessed daughter. So she called out to Him to have mercy on her. At first, Jesus didn't say a word. The disciples wanted to send her away because they were annoyed by her. The silence of Jesus nor the rejection of the disciples, discouraged this great woman of faith. She cried out even more to the Lord to have mercy on her. When Jesus did answer He said, *"I am not sent but to the lost sheep of the house of Israel"* (Matthew15:24). That just made her more determined. She fell at His feet and worshipped Him and pleaded for help.

Jesus replied to her plea by seemingly calling her a dog. She didn't let that stop her. She was willing to eat the crumbs that fell from the Master's table. This woman passed the test of faith so much so that *"Jesus answered and said unto her, O woman, great is they faith: be it unto thee even as thou wilt"* (Matthew 15:27). You can't be a wimp when your faith is being tested. You have to stand on the Word of God and believe that He will deliver on the promise.

Some of you may have not received your blessing because your faith is weak. You flunked the test of faith. Every time things get tough, you coil–up and get into unbelief. Stay in faith! The Bible tells us to live by our faith.

Look at Genesis twenty-two, beginning in verse one, It says, *"and it came to pass after these things that God did **tempt** Abraham."* Now if your Bible, is like mine, where it says *tempt,* just simply write in its place the word **test.** The word *'tempt'* and the word *"test"* mean the same thing. God tested Abraham to see if he would obey and offer up Isaac. It means that God was putting Abraham to the test. He was testing Abraham's faith.

God will test your faith too and if you desire to be whole you will pass the test. You won't mumble, complain and gripe about how hard life is and how you never get the breaks. You'll do as the Apostle James said and **count it all joy and let the trying of your faith develop patience in you.** Patience is the source to getting an answer to your prayer. Let patience have her work in your life.

Faith in God will give you staying power. You won't faint in times of testing. Instead, you will get in agreement with God. So change your confession and begin to say, "I might be down now, but I'm going to rise again." "I may be in a financial mess, but I'll overcome it." "I am whole and everything I need is in Christ."

God wants you to say you are strong. Faith says confess what you believe. Go on, and say "I'm more than a conqueror!" "Whatever is not of faith," the Bible says in Romans fourteen, *"is sin."* The question is, if faith is what makes my life rewarding and fulfilling, how does God build my faith? Can I take vitamins for it? No. Is there some kind of therapy I can go through to have my faith built? No. Then how is it done?

Here's the secret. God builds our faith by testing it. He builds our faith by allowing us to experience certain things, and to go through trials and problems that will reveal to us if we are in faith or not. Speaking from experience Job says, *"What is man that you make so much of him and that you give him so much attention and that you examine him every morning and test him every moment."* (Job 7:17-18). Did you realize that God is testing you every moment of your life? A woman of faith will stand the test.

How God Builds Our Faith

God tests our faith through difficulties. That's trials, problems, pressures, tough circumstances and all the challenges of life.

1 Peter 1:6-7 says, *"For a little while you have had to suffer great and all kinds of trials. These have come so that your faith may be proved genuine and may result in praise, glory and honor when Jesus Christ is revealed."* The trials and the problems and the difficulties that come into your life come to prove your faith.

God tests our faith by asking us to do things that are seemingly impossible. There are many commands for the believer to obey and some of them seem unreasonable. Some of them seem inconvenient. Some of them seem downright impossible for us to do in our own strength. So what do you do when you have an impossible command that feels like a demand? You trust God and remember that you can do all things through Christ who gives you strength.

Money is one of the greatest tests of faith in your life? Few people understand that God uses our material possessions as a test of faith. For many people finances are the greatest test of all. They have no idea that God is actually testing them when they're going through a financial problem. See, when you are asked to give, this has to do with faith. In Luke 16:11 Jesus says this, *"If you haven't been trustworthy in handling worldly wealth, [That's money] who will trust you with true riches?"* Evaluate how much faith your giving reveals. Get gut level honest. If God looked at your giving, could He say that you really trust Him? Or have you not done what His Word says and given a tithe to the work of the ministry? Do you spend money getting your nails and hair done, and buying expensive jewelry then give God what's left?

God tests our faith through **delaying our requests.** If every prayer was instantly answered, if your every need was immediately met, and if every problem was quickly solved you wouldn't need faith. Your faith wouldn't need to be exercised. But it is not that way. We have to wait on things. It is human nature to hate to wait. But waiting is a test of faith.

By faith, you can believe, I'm going to make it. I have the favor of God on my life. God has already solved this problem. God has birthed purpose in me, and I'll fulfill the purpose for which I was created. Believe that the problem you are experiencing is really a blessing turned upside down. As a matter of fact, thank God in the midst of it. Tell Him that you believe He is working on your behalf. The power of belief is tremendous!

If you can thank God when things are bleak, that is a sign of true faith.

So if you want to be a total woman, you must be a woman of faith. If you want to increase in faith, you have to rejoice in the Lord at all times— in both good times and bad. You must be obedient to God's commands, be a giver and learn to wait on God. You can be an example of a woman of faith!

CHAPTER 6
The Woman of Wisdom

"Through wisdom is a house builded; and by understanding it is established: And by knowledge shall the chambers be filled with all precious and pleasant riches" (Proverbs 24:3-4).

A total woman is a wise woman. She has deliberately chosen to acquire God's wisdom. We can never just drift into wisdom. We must seek God and make a conscious decision to receive His wisdom daily. Choosing God's wisdom begins when we realize the value of wisdom. The Bible says, *"For wisdom is better than rubies; and all the things that may be desired are not to be compared to it"* (Proverbs 8:11). **The wisdom of God is priceless!** Wisdom's worth cannot be measured.

Wisdom cannot be reduced to a mere formula. It's the greatest treasure. Wisdom is not learned in the course of days, months, or years. It comes with spiritual maturity. It comes from not just having information about God but through times of testing and proving His faithfulness. God wants us to live life wisely.

The twenty-first century is not an easy time in which to be a wise woman. This time offers women a wider range of possibilities than ever before, but with each choice we make, there are consequences. Therefore, our choices must be weighed carefully. God's Word must be our guide to ensure that our choices are pleasing to Him. Women must examine their beliefs and attitudes about their roles as wives, mothers, and co-workers, as well as the status of their spiritual and personal growth.

We live in a time when the old ways are quickly becoming obsolete and new ideas not based on the Word of God have become the norm. This time is both exciting and frightening. It is exciting because we live in an information age.

It is a time where we can communicate with others all over the world. It is a great opportunity to spread the good news of the Lord Jesus Christ. Today women can make choices that women did not have the opportunity to make years ago. But many of the choices are causing the firm anchor of the old truths to gradually slip away. We need the wisdom of God to help us in our decisions and in our walk with Him.

The Greatest Treasure

So what are the true riches of God that come with wisdom? Paul said that *"all the treasures of wisdom"* are hid in Christ (Colossians 2:3). After we get rid of the old man on the cross, we then are "dead and our life is hid with Christ in God." Our treasure is found in Him. Some have twisted the word "riches" to mean only money: filthy lucre, mammon, riches and wealth of this world. But, I know a greater treasure; it is wisdom. Wisdom is better than silver or gold or riches untold. There are no words to express the riches of wisdom.

I believe one of the greatest needs among God's people is wisdom. To have God's wisdom is to enter the heart of God. Proverbs: 4:7 says, *"Wisdom is the principal thing; therefore get wisdom: and with all thy getting get understanding."* Principle thing means the main thing. That means nothing is more important. Wisdom exalted will fulfill every need. Do you value wisdom? **The things you value will determine your course of life**. When you esteem the important things, you will be willing to give up the temporary things so that you can achieve what God has planned for your life.

King Solomon could have had anything he wanted. God asked him what He should give him. Solomon asked God for wisdom, and God gave it to him. He asked for the greatest gift and received the best gift. He will give you wisdom also, but you must esteem it. You must appreciate its value in your life.

One of my favorite scriptures is found in Proverbs 3: 5-7. It says, *"Trust in the Lord with all thy heart and lean not unto your own understanding, in all thy ways acknowledge him and He shall direct thy* paths. *Be not wise in thine own eyes."* I hear this scripture quoted often, but when quoting it they always stop at verse six. The scripture continues by saying and be not wise in your own eyes. King Solomon tells you to trust in the Lord with all your heart and lean not on your intellect to direct you. You do this by not being wise in your own eyes. In other words, we don't have all the knowledge and understanding we need to direct our paths in life, we need wisdom.   Some people do not prosper, because they lean to their own understanding and do not acknowledge God in their ways. Both must go together to complete being a wise women. I remember when God spoke to me and said, "Carolyn you need wisdom." He was saying I need the Word. I had been making decisions and living my life according to the world's wisdom. In other words, I was a foolish woman. I needed to do things according to the principles of God and not my own way. I was so glad to hear that wisdom came from God and that I could have wisdom. It changed the results I was receiving from the decisions that I made.

Wisdom is the God-inspired system for making right choices. Wisdom will show you how to overcome roadblocks and stumbling blocks that are set up to stop and deter you from making good decisions. There is absolutely no substitute for wisdom and no success without it.

If we arrange our lives around the goal of gaining wisdom,

we will receive rewards that far exceed anything we can think or imagine. **God says nothing compares in value with the spiritual treasures contained in the Word.**

King Solomon said in Proverbs chapter three and verse fifteen that wisdom is better than rubies and all the things that may be desired are not to be compared to it. **Wisdom has the greatest value.** Wisdom is better than fortune, fame, and power, achievement, silver or gold–better than the lottery or hitting the jackpot. WOW!

Wisdom is having an understanding of what is really important! A person of wisdom judges all things, collects evidence, acquires information, weighs the information and compares it with God's Word. A person without wisdom is often deceived by reasoning of the fleshly mind. They govern themselves with an attitude of, "It's my thing baby, and I'll do what I want to do!" They do it their way with no regard of the outcome. One without wisdom usually does not know how to deal with conflict and how to manage the affairs of life successfully.

Often times women without wisdom act immaturely in a crisis and cannot successfully handle the valleys of life. Some will even give up easily in their relationships. The wisdom of God will give you insight and foresight to help you during situations or times when things are very uncertain, difficult or painful. It will give you discernment to see the stumbling block before you stumble. Wisdom will help guide you in relationships so you will be a discerner of what is good or evil. You cannot put a price on wisdom. **It is valuable**!

Where do you find this treasure? I am glad you want to know. It is yours just for the asking. We can receive wisdom by asking God for it. The Bible tells us in James chapter one and verse five, *'If any of you lacks wisdom, let him ask of God, who gives liberally and without reproach, and it will be given to him."* It's just that easy. Ask God to give you wisdom to help you manage the affairs of life. I know people who have an average intelligence, who do not have a dazzling personality, neither outstanding credentials, but are working in important positions. They are successful because they know how to manage themselves wisely. They know how to translate knowledge into wise action!

Wisdom is a system that will help navigate you through life. It is like the compass that the sailors use to direct them on an ocean. It's like the comptroller who directs the pilots in the air. It's like the little light in the light house, which leads the ships in the dark. When you apply the Word of God it will enable you to make wise choices. **There is no greater treasure than wisdom!**

Knowledge is not Wisdom

There is a difference between knowledge and wisdom. I know you are smart – but do you have wisdom? Wisdom is knowing when and how to apply knowledge. Apostle Paul points out in Second Timothy chapter three and verse seven that some people are always learning and never coming to a grasp of the truth.

Paul explained that some learners are never able to obtain the truth because they look to the wrong sources. They go to the internet or other resource materials, even the physics to get information about what they should do in life. They look for answers on who they should marry or what career they should have and many other questions that pertain to successful living. These resources serve useful purposes, but they are not God's Word. You must go to the Bible to find God's truth about your purpose and His direction for your life.

Don't misunderstand me. It is possible to learn a lot from standard reference books written by devoted men and women and still not come to know the divinely-revealed truth that comes from the wisdom of God's Word. There are many who are ever learning but never able to come to the knowledge of the truth because of a wrong attitude toward truth. Some think that to store information in the intellect is all that matters. Many of them study the Bible, and quote scripture after scripture, but they lack the one thing that is indispensable to saving knowledge: the desire to obey God. Jesus said, *"If any man will do his will, he shall know of the doctrine, whether it be of God, or whether I speak of myself"* (John 7:17).

Willingness to do the will of God is essential to knowing the truth. Intellectual understanding avails only when it is applied. You may be able to quote scripture and not know how to relate or apply the meaning of it to yourself. However, James tells us to, *"be ye doers of the word, and not hearers only, deceiving your own selves"* (James 1:22).

Wisdom gives wings to knowledge.

Wisdom is the ability to take the knowledge we receive and apply it. First, we hear and receive the Word of God. Next, revelation comes from what we have heard. With the understanding of that revelation, we become a doer of what we hear. Then that wisdom we operate in will result in manifestation. Wisdom demands that we work with God and according to His plan.

What is Wisdom?

Webster's Dictionary defines the word *"wise"* as: *"having the power of discerning and judging properly as to what is true or right; possessing discernment, judgment or discretion."* Wisdom is the discernment of truth combined with the good judgment to know what is right and how and when to apply the knowledge you have.

When God gives you wisdom you have a responsibility to respond wisely to the things that you discern. True discernment is not given for us to be judgmental or condemning toward others. It is given so we can discern the moving of God's Spirit and follow Him. **True wisdom has an advantage** - it will make your outward affairs prosperous and your life successful. I like to think of wisdom as having a skill for living – it's a **"know how."** It is to know how to take the information and knowledge you receive and apply it appropriately.

There are a lot of people with masters degrees, PhD's and all kinds of educational degrees who do not have wisdom. Wisdom is a necessary and vital ingredient to effectual, productive abundant living.

Principles for Wisdom

The first principle of wisdom is the fear of God, which is the beginning of wisdom. The Bible says in Psalm111:10 *"The fear of the LORD is the beginning of wisdom: a good understanding have all they that do his commandments: his praise endureth for ever."* Fearing God is the first step towards understanding "the knowledge of Divine things." We fear God as a servant fears a master, or we fear God as a child fears a parent. Man must first of all fear (reverence) God and submit to Him. The fear of the Lord is to be God-conscious, and to know what pleases and displeases Him. Knowing God is wise!

The second principle to become wise is to associate with wise people. Stay away from fools because the companion of fools shall be destroyed (Proverbs13:20). Multitudes are brought to ruin by bad company. Many have made bad decisions that have caused them their future and their relationship with their family. My mother use to warn me about keeping bad company or hanging out with the wicked. That was wisdom!

Examples of Wise Women

In 1 Samuel chapter 25 we meet a man name Nabal and his wife Abigail. Nabal was a hard man to live with. He was mean, harsh, overbearing and an evil doer. Nabal was a man with great possessions. Abigail lived in a difficult situation like many of you may be that are reading this book. But, Abigail knew what to do in a difficult situation. The Bible says, Abigail was a woman of good understanding and of a beautiful countenance. Abigail, I might add, has always been one of my favorite women in the Bible, because of her wisdom.

It was sheep shearing season and it was customary for the sheep owner to provide a feast when the job was done, for all who had participated. This was done as an act of gratefulness to God. David sent his men to Nabal to be repaid for the protection they had provided to his shepherds all the year. David sent a salutation of peace and kindness. He could have used his influence or military power, but he didn't. They expected Nabal to be generous, but Nabal refused to give them anything; and he questioned who David was, as if to say David was a "nobody."

When David received the report he was angry. David ordered his men to gird on their swords. He was preparing to carry four hundred men with him to destroy Nabal's household.

One of the young men informed Abigail of her husband's foolish remarks. She realized the danger of the situation and immediately took action. Abigail knew her husband was a fool. His name means "fool". So she took *"two hundred loaves, and two bottles of wine, and five sheep ready dressed, and five measures of parched corn, and an hundred clusters of raisins, and two hundred cakes of figs, and laid them on asses"* (1 Samuel 25:18). Abigail sent her servants ahead of her. I believe she sent them ahead so she could talk to God about the situation. She needed to know what to say to David. She needed wisdom!

When she met David, she spoke with words of wisdom. Listen to her conversation. *"Upon me, my lord, upon me let this iniquity be: and let thine handmaid, I pray thee, speak in thine audience, and hear the words of thine handmaid"* (1 Samuel 25:24). Abigail didn't act angry, boisterous and contentious. She bowed down at David's feet and asked for forgiveness. This was an act of humility. A woman of wisdom is **humble. The total woman is humble but strong.**

I believe God had revealed to Abigail the future of David. In verse twenty eight she says, *"I pray thee, forgive the trespass of thine handmaid: for the Lord will certainly make my lord a sure house; because my lord fighteth the battles of the Lord, and evil hath not been found in thee all thy days."* WOW! David recognized Abigail's good judgment and blessed her for keeping him from bloodshed. Abigail successfully stopped David from destroying her household.

But, how would she handle the situation with her husband. Did she go home and curse him out and tell him what a fool he was and that he almost got them killed? I think not. That would not be wisdom. Remember there was a feast going on, and He was at home drinking. She waited until morning when the feast was over and Nabal was sober. Let me think for a minute. How could she discern the right time to speak to him? I imagine since she was a woman of wisdom, this is probably how she did it. Let's go into her home. She fixed his favorite warm breakfast and set the table with flowers. She also was nicely adorned. She set at the table with him, and in a soft tone of voice, Abigail explained to her husband the seriousness of his behavior.

Abigail was wise. When she needed to confront her husband, she perceived the right time to do so. It is crucial that you discern the appropriate time to confront. Bad timing can be catastrophic. The timing can make a big difference in the outcome. The shock of Nabal's near disaster with David put him into cardiac arrest and within a short period of time he was dead.

When David heard of Nabal's death, he proposed to Abigail and married her.

She was a suitable wife for a king!

Her good judgment earned her a place as the queen. A wise woman rightly assesses a problem and relies upon the Lord to give her the wisdom to address it.

Another wise woman was Jochebed, the mother of Moses. One of the greatest honors given to a woman is to be a mother. There is no greater assignment than that of motherhood. The character she builds in a child's life is her legacy. Jochebed's story tells us that our greatness is measured by what we do with our lives.

In a time when every mother was losing their sons, Jochebed gave birth to Moses. The king had issued an edict to destroy every son born to Hebrew women. She knew that her child was a gift from God, so Jochebed cried out to God when Moses was born. I'm sure Jochebed was powerless against the king, but she knew Who had all power. She prayed and listened for the wisdom of God to give her a strategy for her situation.

Human wisdom has limits. However, God's wisdom is infinite and transcendent. He had a purposeful plan for the child, Moses. Jochebed placed the child in the bulrushes at the edge of the Nile River. Her step of faith and act of wisdom was rewarded. God inclined the heart of Pharoah's daughter to save the child, and He also ordered the situation so that Jochebed, the child's own mother would be his nurse. That's awesome! *"A man's steps are directed by the Lord. "How then can anyone understand his own way"* (Proverbs 20:24). It pays to seek God for wisdom! A foolish woman lacks wholeness because she's void of the wisdom of God.

Jochebed's name is not mentioned in the Hall of Fame among the great women of the Bible.

Her life is mentioned only in connection with the first years of the life of Moses. Yet, her memorable contribution to the world is enormous. Her fame is in the names of her children, Miriam, Aaron and Moses, sisters and brothers called by God to lead His chosen people. Jochebed is an example of a "Total Woman."

Wisdom with our Words

The Scripture admonishes us to keep our words pure and to avoid evil speaking; slander, gossip, and backbiting. If we desire to be women of wisdom, it's imperative that we guard the words which come out of our mouths. James wrote about two kinds of wisdom: wisdom that does not come from heaven, and wisdom that does. One is of God and one is not.

The wisdom which is not from heaven, is earthly and of the devil. It reflects itself through, "envy, jealousy, selfish ambition, and every evil practice" (James 3: 15, 16). He tells us that Godly wisdom which comes from heaven, is "pure, considerate, peace-loving, impartial and sincere" (James 3:17, 18).

James instructs us that the tongue, though small, has the power to kindle great fires, to spread deadly poison and to defile the body. He tells us not to offend or hurt others by our words, then we will be perfect. Man cannot tame the tongue. James helps us with this by giving us the prescription for taming the tongue. He tells us to **submit ourselves to God.** Only God can tame the tongue and help us with the difficulties we have in controlling what we say. Proverbs 18:21 tells us that *"death and life are in the power of the tongue: and they that love it shall eat the fruit thereof."* So what kind of fruit are you eating? In other words, what are the results of your words? Your results are an indication of what you are saying.

A woman can do a great deal of good, or a great deal of harm, both to others and to herself, by the use of her tongue. Some women have caused their own death by a foul tongue or the death of others by a false tongue.

On the contrary, some women have saved their own life, or procured the comfort of it, by a wise tongue.

A wise woman knows when to speak and what to say. *"She opens her mouth with wisdom and in her tongue is the law of kindness…favour is deceitful and beauty is vain, but a woman who feareth the Lord, she shall be greatly praised" (Proverbs 31: 26, 30).* Our tongue can be either our best friend or our worse enemy. Proverbs 21:23 says, *"Whoso keepeth his mouth and his tongue keepeth his soul from troubles."* Our words should be pure so they will edify and uplift others. Our words should be kind and soft spoken. Are you creating good in your life by your words or are you causing trouble? Our daily prayer should be: **Lord, set a watch over my tongue.**

Build Your House

The Bible tells us it's "*Through wisdom a house is built; and by understanding it is established: And by knowledge shall the chambers be filled with all precious and pleasant riches*" (Proverbs 24:3-4). A house is built by wisdom,

and the home becomes strong through good understanding. Through knowledge its rooms are filled with all sorts of precious riches and valuables. There is a direct correlation between BUILDING A HOUSE and WISDOM! King Solomon gives us a formula for building and establishing our home. He tells us that in order to build our house and fill it with beautiful things, we need wisdom, understanding and knowledge! Through wisdom a house is built, a family is built up, and it is furnished and supplied with the necessities and conveniences of life. Through understanding the home is brought into flourishing and prosperous circumstances by wise prudent management and diligence. Through knowledge the total woman knows how to care for the family, the home and its contents. She knows how to set an environment of love, peace and comfort.

To be a "Total Woman" you need wisdom!

CHAPTER 7
The Woman of Purpose

"For I know the thoughts that I think to ward you, saith the LORD, thoughts of peace, and not of evil, to give you an expected end" (Jeremiah 29:11).

God created you for a purpose. There is joy in finding the reason for which you were born. God made you unique for His divine purpose. He doesn't make junk, and He doesn't make replicas. He only makes originals. Everything about you is perfectly suited for the purpose for which you were created. You were born into a certain family, are of a certain race, have a certain stature and have a distinctive personality because it complements your purpose. God makes no mistakes, so you are no accident. He made you because He wants you to do something in the earth realm. He pre-selected your date of birth, your race, your sex and your personality.

But maybe you are as I once was, asking yourself these questions:

- **The question of existence - Why am I alive?**
- **The question of significance - Does my life matter?**
- **The question of intention - What is my purpose in life?**

I hope as we continue to take a closer look at purpose, you'll be able to answer these most important questions. Let's begin by answering the question: **How do you define "purpose"?**

Purpose is *being* and *doing* what God intends us to be and do. It's being obedient to what God asks us to do in our family, church, and community; being Christ-like; and then doing the specific work God designed us to do while we are here on earth. But you say, "Okay," but how am I to know what I was designed to do? Is my purpose the same as every other woman's? How do I know when I am living in my purpose? These are valid questions that I hope we can answer.

God made you and if you want to know why something is created, you must ask the one who made it. No one else knows. Thus, go to God and ask Him why did He make you and then make the pursuit of purpose a priority for your life. Actively, search for ways to fulfill the purpose God has for your life. You'll never really be successful without knowing why on earth you are here. So be determined that you're going to get pregnant with purpose! I am, and I love it!

You should pray specifically for God to reveal to you your purpose. You should meditate on pertinent scriptures, such as Psalm 37:4, Jeremiah 29:11, Matthew 14:27, and John 17:1.

I encourage you to clear away some of the mental and emotional clouds that may block you from His revelation.

Indicators of Purpose

Your **passion** will give you a clue to what you were made to do. For example, let's say you have a passion to help people. You get a deep satisfaction from assisting other people with their problems. Chances are your purpose is tied to the service or hospitality and most likely your dominated spiritual gifts are in the area of helps.

Don't get caught in the status trap believing that one profession is more important than another. Without the patient, the doctor would not be needed, without a student, the teacher would be unnecessary, without sanitation workers our health would be at risk, without members of the church, the pastor would not be needed and without intercessors we would be left open to the devil's devises. Every spiritual and natural gift is needed in the kingdom.

Personality is also an indicator of one's purpose. If you are one who loves to interact with people or if you are a great communicator, God made you that way for the reason He created you. That child that talks all the time may very well have been made to teach, preach or entertain others. God has a special purpose for the quiet unassuming child and even the child that is self-reliant, stubborn and hard to deal with. Your personality is suitable for the purpose for which you were created.

Your natural talents and skills will also aid you in discovering what you were created to do. A talented musician makes music. He thrives on making music. He loves music. That's what he was born to do, but how he does it is another matter. Does he glorify God with his gift is the question? You can be publicly acclaimed for your talent and still not be living out your purpose in God. That's the real challenge for multi-talented or extremely talented individuals.

Spiritual gifts are signs of what God has designed you to do. You can find a discussion of the five-fold ministry gifts in Ephesians 4:11, a list of spiritual gifts in 1 Corinthians chapter twelve and other gifts in Romans twelve. It is well worth taking the time to study them. For example, my dominant spiritual gift is preaching. That's also my passion. Awake me at midnight, and I'll start preaching to you God's Word. It's a labor of love. My other spiritual gifts are the gift of healing, deliverance and prophecy. My husband also operates in the gifts of healing and administration. I had never been as excited as when I found out I had spiritual gifts that I could use to make a difference in the kingdom of God. Your gifts help to identify you and help to complete your wholeness.

Discovering Your Gifts

I highly encourage you, if you have not already done so, to make a conscientious effort to discover your spiritual gifts. The Body of Christ needs your gift. There are several instruments for assessing your gifts in the form of spiritual gift inventories. The Holy Spirit blessed us with gifts so that we will edify the Body and minister to the world. Yes, you are a minister. Perhaps, you thought the only ministers were in the pulpit. But God has ministers in every place. They are not only in the church but in the family, community, sports, education, business, arts, entertainment and government. His desire is that we use our gifts to let others know about His love.

Now don't misunderstand me. This is not a license for you to hold a Bible study or preach to others on the job when you should be working. It is an invitation for you to let your light shine so that God will be glorified. Let's say for the sake of clarification, that you have the gift of the Word of Knowledge (specific information given by the Holy Spirit) and the company is looking to expand the business and build a new facility. The activation of your gift may be just the answer they need to find the land to build on. In this case, using your spiritual gift would be an asset to the company. This knowledge can be used to display the work of God in the marketplace without others even realizing what prompted you to provide the information.

Many gifted people live meaningless lives. At the expense of finding the reason why they were born, their whole existence is centered on things that enhance the flesh. **If you are not living a purpose-driven life, you are not living a victorious life. Victory is in God!** We were born to glorify God. That's our life's ultimate goal. He created each of us for a specific earthly assignment, and your success is contingent upon you being who God created you to be. So assess your spiritual and natural skills, talents and gifts and submit them to God for His use.

Born with a Purpose

A hammer was made to hit a nail. It may be used for other purposes, but it was created to nail a nail. God designed you to do a specific thing. But, you can live your entire life pleasing the desires of the flesh and go to the grave without knowing the reason why you were born. That would be a tragedy. No matter what the task or what you accomplish in this life, you still will have not known true success without having fulfilled your purpose in God.

Don't buy into the untruth that you are here on planet earth by accident or that your birth was just an act of nature. Your father's sperm united with your mother's egg and conception occurred, but friend, God knew you before you were conceived. Did He not tell Jeremiah, *"Before I formed thee in the belly, I knew thee; and before thou camest forth out of the womb I sanctified thee, and I ordained thee a prophet unto the nations"* (Jeremiah1:5). Don't think that just because Jeremiah was a prophet, God knew him, and since you are not a prophet, He doesn't know you. Remember, He is All-Knowing! God knew you before you were born, and He had a purpose for you just like He had a purpose for Jeremiah.

Woman with a Purpose

Every woman on planet earth needs to answer the question: **Why on earth am I here?** You are not here without a reason. When God created you He had something that He wanted you to do that no one else on earth could do in His kingdom. Let's go to the Bible and see if we can find an example of a woman who fulfilled her purpose. Mary, the mother of Jesus, immediately comes to mind. She was a woman with a world-changing purpose. She was born to birth the Savior. I know that because it had been prophesied many years before Jesus was born that He would be born of a virgin girl. When the angel Gabriel appeared to Mary to give her the news, at first she was perplexed.

In addition to wondering how it could be since she was a virgin, most likely, Mary thought "who me?" "I'm just a peasant girl." But because she was willing to receive her purpose and embrace her purpose, she dramatically changed the world. Mary's response to her purpose was, *"Behold the handmaid of the Lord; be it done unto me according to thy word…"* (Luke 1:38). Is that your response to the purpose God has for you?

Mary was a woman just like you with like passions. She was often anxious, tried and sad, so don't try to make her into a superwoman, for she was not. **She was blessed among women, not above women**, because she birthed the Savior of the world. But Mary had to live out her life the same as you do.

Mary fulfilled her purpose, and God wants you to do the same. Now, you will never be called to do what Mary did, but whatever God has called you to is very significant. When He formed you in your mother's womb He had a definite purpose for your life. Even though, you can't birth the Savior you may very well birth the one who cures cancer, or you, yourself, may discover a cure for one of the world's greatest ills or share valuable knowledge with the world in a way that no one else can. Thus, pursue your purpose.

Pursuing Life's Purpose

As you pursue your purpose, ask yourself some defining questions. The first being: **What matters most to you?** Perhaps you enjoy working with teenagers, feeding the hungry, working in a nursery, teaching a foreign language, loving the poor or pioneering a new business. Aligning with God's purpose doesn't necessarily mean you won't work in a secular job. God may allow you to be the most effective through your secular work for a lifetime, or he may use your work for a season and then call you into a different place of service. Therefore, be sure you have asked, "What matters most to me?"

God's desire is for you to know what it is He has assigned you to do. Don't just coast along in life without a definite purpose. I hear too many women say, "Child, I'm just trying to get by. I'm barely making it." It's evident that they have not tapped into the purpose God has for them. I recommend that you search your heart, read God's Word, pray, and spend time in the area of service that you most care about. If you still lack clarity, ask your pastor, a family member, a co-worker, a teacher or a few trusted friends for their input.

The next question you should ask yourself is: **What do you want your life to count for?** Few people are ever remembered for more than two or three significant areas where they made a lasting difference. It is helpful to know what those areas are for you and to get focused on them. Have you ever heard the phrase, "Jack of all trades, Master of none?" That's a description of some people because they never horned in on their dominant skills. So, focus in on your dominant gifts.

I encourage you also to consider another key question: **"How do I want to be remembered?"** Through the things you do—even the routine things. Remember the only thing you will leave that will last is what you did for Christ.

View life's purpose from an eternal perspective. Then, ask God to make your life count, not only in familiar things but in new ways that you have never imagined. When I asked myself this question, I was surprised at my answer. I want to be remembered for helping someone to find their purpose in life, for having compassion toward others and for being a witness for Christ. Glory! This is what wholeness is about! Another question you should ask yourself is: **How is the purpose that God has for my life relevant to other people?**

As you pursue God's purpose for your own life, consider how that purpose relates to God, family, friends, and to others. God is in the people business, and His purpose for your life never omits bringing Him glory or caring for others. The apostle Paul noted in Romans 15:16 that God had appointed him *"to be a minister of Christ Jesus to the Gentiles."* This was Paul's specific calling and the way he fulfilled God's purpose for his life. As a result of his passion to fulfill that purpose, the world was eternally changed.

Perhaps you are asking, "If God has a purpose for me, why do I often feel as though I'm simply going through the motions of living? Most likely, that is because you're in "robot mode." We let busyness, fear, or impure motives drive out our purpose. We try hard to work at becoming holy in the day-to-day grind instead of experiencing the reward of fulfilling the reason God put us on earth. Most of us are more concerned with religious obligations than with unearthing the buried passion God put in us. We rarely stop to ask: Am I doing what God wants me to do? Am I living out my purpose? As women, it is important that we discover our purpose in life for three reasons. First, fulfilling our purpose in life gives glory to God. Second, it releases us from the captivity of despair. Thirdly, it completes us.

But to discover our more unique life mission, we must be willing to move forward and not look back. We can't let the circumstances surrounding our birth such as who our parents are, where we were born, or our past history to hinder us. **What do you mean?**

Paul writes, *"Brethren, I count not myself to have apprehended: but this one thing I do, forgetting those things which are behind, and reaching forth unto those things which are before, I press toward the mark for the prize of the high calling of God in Christ Jesus"* (Philippians 3:13-14). Many of us numb the pain caused by the deep unhealed wounds from the past through self-medication, busyness, overspending, and doing "good stuff" and the pain becomes our purpose.

Past influences have a big effect on our everyday life. We have to put anger, regret, bitterness, and pain behind us before we can focus on the race God has set before us. It's difficult to hear God's voice over the noise and confusion in which we live. Many of us need a more mature Christian to help shed light on what God was saying to us about His will for our life.

We can't be a lone ranger in the purpose discovery process? A woman trying to find her life purpose alone is like a novice trying to pastor a church. Both need a partner who can prepare them for the challenges and risks that lie ahead.

Many women fail to fulfill their life purposes because they have no mentor or adviser to help them reach the next mile marker. God designed our purpose to happen in a community—whether it's in person, online, through a telephone relationship, letter writing, or as an intercessory prayer warrior. Giving and receiving love is part of God's design and nothing can substitute for it.

Yes, God wants to bring spiritual friendships into our lives. The Christian community can happen anywhere there is group fellowship. Each of us need someone to keep us accountable to God's call on our life. We need to be in a group where we can be authentic and safe. Because of the dangers of a "lone ranger" lifestyle, we must rely on others to walk alongside us. "I need you and you need me." No one is ever successful alone.

Is there a difference between purpose and passion?

Our *purpose* is to be a woman of God and do what He asks us to do. Our *passions* are godly indicators that help us to identify our purpose. For example, my passions include preaching, reading, decorating, traveling and hanging out with my daughter and grandchildren. God's purpose for me is to help transform lives through His Word and to convey to others the practicality of His Word and how to apply it to their lives.

How can we embrace God's purpose, especially if it is not exciting or what we hoped it would be?

Every purpose in God is important. The Bible tells us that if we give a drink of water to someone in need that's important in the sight of God. He created you, and He knows what you are best suited to do. You'll never be happier than you are when you are living out your purpose in God. Don't covet someone else's purpose. Instead do what God has called you to do. Many women in the kingdom don't know how to stay in their lane. Instead, they want to do what God has assigned for someone else to do.

The best way I've found to guard against jealousy over someone else's gift or ministry is to invite God to reveal His vision for *your* life. Then believe with all your heart, He'll do so. If you find yourself envying others, confess it to God; pray for the person's success; and support them in their endeavors. When another sister wins, you win! That's not a popular idea today in the world, but it is with God, because we are a part of one another.

What's the importance of purposeful living?

The most important thing is that you complete your mission and the work that the Lord Jesus gave you to do. God takes anyone who is willing to do His will—no matter how broken or scared they are. He weaves every thread of your life into His quilt of love, even our hurts and failures, and He specializes in second chances.

God uses adversity to give us the substance we need to make our purpose in Him richer. He heals our hurts and comforts us so that we can offer the same hope to other women. He provides for us every day. The ordinary hum-drum routines of life—no matter what they are—can provide staggering opportunities to help others to realize that they are important to God.

In the end, purposeful living is about hope. It will keep hope alive and help you realize that God does have a plan for your life. As the Bible promises in Jeremiah 29:11, *"For I know the thoughts that I think toward you, saith the LORD, thoughts of peace, and not of evil, to give you an expected end."*

You are a daughter of destiny! You are destined to be a "Total Woman!

Don't Procrastinate

Woman of God, God has a purpose for your life, and it's not just to live day after day without a vision. The Bible tells us that without a vision we perish. Living in purpose is the only way to live. If you are not living in God's purpose and living by God's design, then you are not really alive. Purpose gives meaning to life. Purpose motivates and gives direction to our lives. God didn't make you just to hang around feeling blue and wishing you would meet Mr. Right or to be a woman with-out significance. He made you to soar like an eagle! So stop letting appearance, lack of education, family background and social status stop you from being who God called you to be. All those things can be altered. You can change how you look, upgrade your education, overcome the limitation of your background and step up.

Don't let another day pass without living in purpose. God may not give you a full explanation of why He created you to do a certain thing. But whatever He has asked you to do, do it without hesitation. **Delayed obedience is disobedience.** So stop procrastinating and get busy trusting that God knows what's best for you. The reason you want to live out your purpose is for the glory of God. The night before they crucified Jesus, He reported to His Father, *"I have glorified you on earth: I have finished the work which thou gavest me to do"* (John 17:4). God wants you to live out your purpose. **The Total Woman is one who lives on purpose, in purpose and for a purpose**!

CHAPTER 8
I'm Every Woman

"Who can find a virtuous woman? For her price is far above rubies" (Proverbs 31:10).

We come into the kingdom as we are and God transforms us to be the women we are destined to be. **We are daughters of the King**! We have the privilege and the responsibility to represent Him in every area of our lives. Don't allow the enemy to hold you back. Accept your identity and walk in it! You are created "to do all things through Christ who strengthens you." Look at yourself through the eyes of the King. See yourself as He sees you. God does not see any imperfections or failures, but He sees His daughters as beautiful!

To Him you are special, because you were created as an expression of Him. You are full of potential and designed to accomplish great works, for the Kingdom and for His Glory. I encourage you to acknowledge your divine identity as a daughter of the King and to see and know your value. God made no mistakes when He formed you. **You can be whole in every area!**

So, take the mask off. Tear away all the unnecessary baggage and restrictions that are hindering that "every woman" from coming forth. Let the real you take the stage in your life. Give yourself permission to be you. I did and I love it! The scriptures in Proverbs 31 paints a very definitive picture of a **total woman** who raises a family, is a successful wife, runs a business, ministers to others, and manages a household, all at the same time. She was not superwoman, just a virtuous woman. This woman did it all with grace and success! You can too.

A Woman of Love, not fear

"For God hath not given us the spirit of fear; but of power, and of love, and of a sound mind" (2 Timothy 1:7).

God has given us the power by the Holy Spirit to be free from **ALL** fears. The scriptures are clear that God is not the author of fear, but of love. Fear is a stronghold that will hinder your life! Many women have: fear of success, fear of death, fear of the devil, fear of a godly home, fear of being alone, and the list goes on and on. We have to identify and confront our fears.

The Bible tells us in I John 4:18-21 *"There is no fear in love; but perfect love casteth out fear: because fear hath torment. He that feareth is not made perfect in love. We love him, because he first loved us. If a man say, I love God, and hateth his brother, he is a liar: for he that loveth not his brother whom he hath seen, how can he love God whom he hath not seen? And this commandment have we from him, That he who loveth God love his brother also."*

The beloved John tells us that God is love, and the woman whose life is lived in love does, in fact, live in God, and God does, in fact, live in her. Our love for Him grows more and more. As our love grows it fills us with complete confidence of His love for us. For we must realize that our life in this world is actually His life lived in us. **Love contains no fear** - indeed fully-developed love expels every particle of fear. The woman that lives in fear has not yet had her love perfected in Christ.

We cannot hate our sisters and claim to love God. If you hate on your sister especially those of the household of faith, then you're not walking in love and your walk is not pleasing to God. As a matter of fact, it makes you a liar. The apostle John tells us, if a man says, *"I love God" and hates his brother, he is a liar."* My sisters, God gives us an explicit command that the one who loves Him must love her sister also. Become a true sister! Love one another in spite of our differences or challenges. **The total woman knows how to walk in love and demonstrates that love through her actions.**

Knowing that God loves me unconditionally frees me from mistreating and judging others. Love is that power which inspired my life and led me to discover my purpose. Everything hangs on God, Who is love. Endeavor to be a woman with a heart full of love. Let that love overflow to another sister! *"Give, and it shall be given unto you; good measure, pressed down, and shaken together, and running over, shall men give into your bosom. For with the same measure that ye mete withal it shall be measured to you again"* (Luke 6:38). When we give love, we shall ourselves reap the benefit of it. When God recompenses, He recompenses abundantly!

A Woman of Prayer

"I love the LORD, because he hath heard my voice and my supplications. Because he hath inclined his ear unto me, therefore will I call upon him as long as I live" (Psalm 116: 1-2).

God wants to be intimate with us! He wants us to call unto Him. He longs to fellowship with us, to refresh us, and to encourage us. God is always ready to listen to His children. We can come to Him at any time! We have the freedom to call whenever, about anything, and about anyone.

King David said he loved the Lord, because He had heard his prayers. He said he will pray to Him as long as he lives. I will too. God is committed to answering when we call. He wants to impart spiritual strength and encourage us on our journey of life. Prayer is an opportunity to receive from the Lord and a time to yield to

His way. Many of us look at prayer as a means of getting things for ourselves and that is true, but prayer is also a way that we get to know God.

Faith is a necessary element for our prayers to be answered. Faith is belief, trust and confidence in God. Paul says in Ephesians that we have bold and confident access to God through faith in Christ Jesus (Ephesians 3:12). Unwavering faith in God is essential to answered prayers.

A total woman understands the power of prayer. She does not pray just when there is a crisis in her life, but she has a lifestyle of prayer. She recognizes that all her strength and joy comes from spending time in His presence.

As a matter of fact, she loves to pray. She does not find it to be a hard task but a pleasurable one.

It has been a discipline of mine to pray in the Spirit early in the morning and late at night. I choose a set of scriptures to pray and ask God to make His Word a part of my life. Throughout the day, I meditate on those scriptures. The woman, who prays and meditates upon the Word, knows the secret of prayer is praying in the Spirit.

There are many benefits to developing a prayer life. It deepens your relationship with God and will help you to grow spiritually. **Prayer makes us sensitive to the voice of the Holy Spirit**.

When I started communing with Him in prayer, my ability to hear His voice became clearer. Through hearing of His voice, we can follow and obey Him without hesitation. Because it gives us a greater assurance that His Spirit is leading us. **Prayer will increase our faith**. The more you pray the more your faith will grow. I have witnessed God answer my prayers over and over again. Receiving an answer to your prayers encourages you to continue to pray. **Prayer will provide a place for us to unload our troubles and struggles**. You don't have to dump your problems on your girlfriend. You have the Heavenly Father waiting to listen. Peter tells us in 1 Peter 5:7 to *"cast all our cares upon Him, for He careth* *for us."* **Prayer changes things and changes lives.** I can truly say that prayer will change you. During my times of struggle and disappointments, I found that God was very near. Through prayer, He not only changed my situations, but I was changed as well. **Prayer will help us to kill the sin nature and become a pure and holy vessel.** If we confess our sins during our prayer time, The Holy Spirit will purge us of things that are wrong in our lives, and strengthen us to live holy. It is a joy to go to the Father in prayer!

A Woman of Vision

Proverbs 29:18 says, *"Without a vision, the people perish."* **The total woman is a woman of vision.** Her life is motivated and focused by that vision. Having vision refers to the ability to grasp the mind and will of God for your life. Vision enables us to see the "big picture" rather than getting stuck in the now. When I think about vision I think about a puzzle, lying on the table with all the pieces. Vision sees the result of the pieces being put together to make it a whole.

Vision is seeing with our spirit man what is to be in the natural. We see with our eyes, but vision is with our spirit. I remember as a girl when I worked in the cotton field, I had a vision of owning a clothing store. I could see taking that cotton and making it into beautiful dresses. I could see it very clearly in my heart. With wisdom, focus, and determination that vision came to pass!

I love the eagles! They have great vision. **All birds have eyes – but eagles have vision.** The eagle can see beyond its present circumstances and can see several hundred miles away. He does not judge things by what he sees up close. When you don't have vision, you will judge everything by what you see naturally. The eagle can see both forward and to the side at the same time. They have vision and not just sight! God wants us to have vision. In His Word, He tells us that of all the birds of the air, it is the eagle that His people are to be identified with. He is calling us to be "spiritual eagles." The eagle stands upon the rock and can see a great distance. The rock that the Eagle Christian stands upon is the Word of God.

Proverbs 23:26 says, *"Let thine eyes observe my ways."* God wants us to see by faith the vision that He has for us.

Unlike most animals, eagles do well in storms. Most animals seek out a place to hide during the storm. But the eagle will fly right out into the midst of a storm, because he can see something the other animals cannot see. He will look up to where he last saw the sun. The clouds, the rain, the lightning and the loud thunder won't distract him. Because he has vision and his eyes are set upon the sun.

When the storm becomes intense, that's when the eagle mounts up in that storm and flies right to where he last saw the sun. All of a sudden, he breaks through the storm, and the sun begins to dry his feathers. When we have vision, we won't run in a time of difficulty, but we'll look to the Son, Jesus Christ. **The Total Woman has the vision to see the Son during trials and difficulties.**

God spoke to Abraham when his circumstances looked impossible. At nearly one hundred years of age, it looked like he and Sarah would not have a child, and in the natural it was impossible. **Yet, God said, look at the stars!** God had to change Abrah's vision. God wanted him to see in the spirit what He saw. He wanted him to have the eyes of faith. **Without a vision, you will perish.** Webster defines *perish* as to die; to waste away; to decay; to be destroyed. So that means our life is futile without a vision.

Vision is having intelligent foresight, or imaginary sight with the ability to envision the possible future. **The Total Woman has a vision and can see images and dreams in her heart!**

A Woman of Freedom

> *"Therefore seeing we also are compassed about with so great a cloud of witnesses, let us lay aside every weight, and*

the sin which doth so easily beset us, and let us run with patience the race that is set before us"(Hebrews 12: 1-2).

The Bible tells us to lay aside the encumbrances that keep us from running or progressing in our spiritual lives. The Israelites were freed from the bondage of the Egyptians, yet they still longed for the food they received while in Egypt. They were willing to become slaves again to satisfy their flesh. **True freedom is realizing that apart from Christ, you are not free**.

The story of Ruth is one of freedom. There was a famine in the land and because of the famine, the Israelite Elimelech took his wife, Naomi, and their two sons and fled the land of Judah for Moab. Moab was a place of idolatry. Naomi's two sons married heathen wives, Oprah and Ruth. They lived in Moab for ten years. Elimelech and his two sons died. In Judah, the famine was over and word came to Naomi that God was once again visiting His people with plenty. Naomi and her two daughters-in-law started the journey to Judah, a place where God was visiting His people. They were being drawn by the Spirit and grace of the Lord. Naomi's name means "grace." The sad thing is that Oprah and Ruth would be faced with a decision. When they reached the border, Naomi told them to return to their mother's houses *"that you may find rest"* (Ruth 1:9). Their decision would require more than emotions. They would have to make a decision of faith. Oprah and Ruth remained steadfast, at least on the surface. They lifted up their voices and wept. In spite of Oprah's river of tears and her strong words, she returned to her idolatry. Outwardly she was sad and broken and she seemed to want to be free of her pass and idolatry. But her heart was saddened by her love for her old friends and family. Oprah did not and could not cut the ties to Moab. She loved her sister Ruth and her mother-in-law Naomi, but her inner struggle would not let her go on. Naomi tested Oprah and Ruth when she said *"Turn back, my daughters; why will you go with me? Are there still sons in my womb, that they may be your husbands? Turn back, my daughters, go"* (Ruth 1: 11-12). Naomi knew that Oprah could not let go of her world and the pass to want the Lord's fullness. She remained bound by the sin of Moab.

The Total Woman is a woman of freedom!

God calls us to give up the "old self", or anything that will hinder our race. We have to grasp the truth that we have been given the power to lay aside any encumbrances. Apostle Paul anxiously tells us that we should run that we may obtain. He points to certain burdens and impediments which he foresees will hinder us and he says, *"Let us lay aside every weight."* We cannot win if we are weighted down—we cannot keep up with the swift race with weights to carry. Without weights, we shall find the spiritual race easier to run and at a swifter pace that is beyond our natural powers.

But weighted, we are doomed to failure. We are to lay aside all worries, cares, fretfulness, ambition, anger, bitterness, greed, and selfish desires! Women, we have to strip ourselves of anything or anyone that weighs us down and hinder our purpose. Consider the hot air balloon. It is designed to rise up and fly high. When the pilot wants to keep it on the ground, he fills the basket with weights, and when he does not want it to go anywhere, he ties it down. When it is time to rise up, they throw the weights out of the basket. Then he lights the fire, and the fire heats the air up. The air inside the balloon gets lighter; and as it gets lighter, it begins to rise up. We are like the balloon, we cannot rise when we are weighed or tied down by the cares of the world.

Take inventory of your closet; be sure you are not carrying someone's baggage. We must lay aside even the weight of pleasing other people. It is difficult to run if you are looking around to see who is pleased with your performance. To be bound by the feelings of others is a weight. Therefore, free yourself of the opinion of others!

I encourage you to lay aside all bitterness, rage, anger, animosity, spitefulness, threats and insults. These are emotions that will hinder your race. God wants you to run confidently and free! **The Total Woman will heed the caution and "lay aside every weight," whether it is great or small,** and press towards the mark! Let me tell you… it really feels good to be FREE!

A Woman with Right Priorities

It is important to have the right priorities in your life. We have to establish the things that are of most importance to us. I will share with you my guidelines that I follow for my life. Remember it's all a part of being a "Total Woman". Priority number one is my personal relationship with God. I love spending time with Him. Priority number two is spending time with my husband and family. God created the family first. Danny and I have date night as often as possible. It's Lovely! We also make sure that we spend time with our daughter and grandchildren. Those grand's will remember the words of wisdom that we share and the time spent with them.

Priority number three is the ministry. I consider it an honor to be used by God. But, He also wants my priorities to be in order. God anoints me to be a servant of honor for Him. My next priority is self, my home and recreation. I take time for myself. It is important to take self-evaluations, rest and exercise. I take a couple of hours each week that are just mine. During that time, I read, shop, work in the yard and just listen to myself. Of course, I take time to enjoy the beauty of God's creation and appreciate the beautiful flowers that He created. **The Total Woman takes time to care for her home.**

When a woman chooses to be a wife and a mother she chooses a God-ordained role. God's plan is that her priority be her home, (Genesis 3: 16-19). The married woman who wants to be in the will of God will make her home a priority and take care of it with pleasure. She will enjoy preparing food and making her home comfortable for her husband and children. Her home will be a home of cleanliness and peace, serving the Lord. If you are a single woman, there is a great deal of freedom in how you care for your home; the importance is that you do. Remember, it is not just being a mother or wife that brings fulfillment, but being a woman of love, faith, and holiness.

There is peace in having your priorities in the right place. God will always bless when we follow His plan. Seek His priority for your life. Your time with Him is the strength of your life.

The Bible says. "*Teach us to number our days, that we may apply our hearts unto wisdom*" (Psalm 90:12). Be careful not to allow other people, your problems, agendas or Satan's plans to deter you and steal your time. You cannot recycle time. I encourage you to take the time to use your time wisely and most effectively. **Right priorities are important to being a "Total Woman."**

Wholesome Relationships

Many of us have some kind of idea in our minds about how a "good" or "happy" relationship is supposed to be. Sometimes we cause ourselves needless suffering. We do this by comparing our own relationships with our idea or someone else's definition of what a relationship should be like. From this comparison we conclude that our own relationship is defective.

Driven by our personal history, our need, and our sight we tend to choose partners who help us meet our present needs and fulfill our expectations. We often choose partners who can help us to work through our issues and grow in the directions in which we desire to grow.

Sometimes we even choose partners who will help us to ease our pains and sorrows.

We all know some couples who seem so mismatched that we wonder how they ever got together. Yet, there is something that holds them together and they enjoy each other and live happily. Other couples seem so devoted to mutual punishment that we wonder how they stay together. Still others, by contrast, appear to be the perfect couple until we hear they're getting a divorce. A woman who is whole in her life knows how to manage a healthy relationship with her spouse, her friends and her co-workers. What does the Bible tell us about godly relationships? Let's explore and see.

From the very beginning, God loved relationships. He created Adam and Eve to have a one on one relationship with Him and also with each other. Relationships have to do with how we're connected to and how we respond to one another. We are either connected to each other; by blood, by marriage or by our associations.

One of the areas in a woman's life that she often has struggles with is her relationships. Through many of my counseling sessions over the years, relationship problems has been one of the 'big ones." As a woman, we were taught how to drive, how to cook, sew and even iron. But who taught us how to have a healthy relationship with our spouse, our children and other females? To have a wholesome relationship we must know how to relate and how to talk to each other. Our behaviors and character must be mature spiritually, so we will act properly towards one another. How you treat others is usually a reflection of your relationship with the Father.

Our relationship with the Lord may not always be what it should be; and when there is a breakdown in our relationship upwardly, there will also be a breakdown in our relationship outwardly - with those around us.

Our Emotions

The Bible teaches us God knows everything we do and say. God knows – and has always known everything about you. He created you with emotions. But we so often let our emotions get the best of us. One minute we are enjoying our life and the next minute we are ready to crucify everyone around us. We have to control our emotions because our emotions can sometimes be deceiving. Emotions have no brain, just feelings; they don't major in theology or godliness. I know your emotions are what makes you human, but don't let them be in charge of how you treat others. The ups and downs in our emotions are one of the major tools Satan uses to steal our peace. Our emotions will come and go. Life is no fun when it is controlled by feelings. Our feelings cannot be trusted because they change from moment to moment. Ladies, depending on what time of the month it is, emotions can be destructive on your relationships. Emotions can be contagious. Don't feed on your bad emotions but feed on your good emotions. Don't let the devil use your feelings to hurt others, he likes to get you operating in the flesh or "soulish" realm. There was a time in my life when I did not resist the negative emotions and, as a result I had a miserable life. I have learned not to allow my feelings to dictate to me and make me response rudely to others. I made a decision to not to respond to those strange feelings or negative thoughts that made me anger every day. I refuse to live on an emotional rollercoaster where my feelings are going up and down from one minute to the next. I do as Paul said, and I think on good things, happy things and godly things! **Control your emotions instead of your emotions controlling you.**

Often I meet ladies who are unkind and unfriendly. Proverbs 18:20 says, *"A man that hath friends must shew himself friendly."* Let me ask you a question? Are you kind to those around you, or are people happier to see you go than to come? Kindness is about caring genuinely for others and doing something to help them. When you are okay with yourself, you can treat everyone with politeness, even those who are rude to you - not because they are nice, but because you are. My grandmother used to say, "kindness does not cost you anything, but can add everything."

The famous preacher, Charles Swindoll once said, *"Kindness is a language that deaf people can hear and that blind people can see."* How do you treat your sisters? Are you rude and arrogant - yes, I said it, arrogant! We build godly relationships by being humble. The Bible has a lot to say about being humble. A humble person is someone who does not boast or try to impress others. Don't be so prideful because your struggle is not what another sister's is. Remember it is only the grace of God that has blessed us to be where we are.

Pride makes everyone around sick, except the one who has it.

Don't look down on those who may not have come out of their storm yet. Remember it is not how you start the race but how you finish it. I remember when I was going to college there were several young female students who talked about me because I did not have a car, or the stylish clothes that they wore. I was a working student. Sometimes their actions toward me made me feel inferior and not worthy to be with them. But I knew that God's purpose for me was filled with eternal significance.

Years later, I met one of those former classmates. She was surprised to see how God has blessed my life. See, the Lord knows who you are and whose you are and who you were designed to be. So don't allow the mistreatment of others to cause you to be unkind. Have a forgiving heart. The human tendency is when someone hurts us we hold grudges, malice, resentment and bitterness or we simply adopt a cold attitude towards that person.

Forgiving is when we can let go of all those attitudes and move forward in loving kindness. We can never move forward unless or until we become a forgiving person. In this life, nearly everyone has been hurt by someone; even Jesus was hurt by His disciples and His own people; but what did He do? On the cross, He said, "Father, forgive them." **To have healthy relationships we must be willing to forgive**.

Apostle Paul reminds us in 1 Corinthians 15:33 to *"Be not deceived: evil communications corrupt good manners."* In this scripture Paul uses the word, *"communications"* to mean being together; companionship; or close contact. No matter how much you want friends you must choose your friends carefully because they will affect you. Some will affect you for evil, and some for good. "Be not deceived" could also be translated as do not roam or wander from the truth. That is what deceivers do. They use their charm and wit to lure you into thinking something evil is good. They learn their skill from Satan who is the first deceiver.

Paul is warning the Corinthians that they are being deceived or tempted to wander from the truth by some people that seem skilled in the Word and holy in their actions. They seem to be the kind of friends and teachers that you need, but they have no character, which is what the word evil means here. I have seen it happen often in the ministry. Sisters befriend one another; enter into a covenant relationship, only to find out that the person's character is not what they portrayed. Be careful of who you allow to enter your inner circle. Remember there were twelve disciples. But, only three were in the inner circle with Jesus-Peter, James, and John. Jesus knew which of the disciples would fit into that close inner circle. Be real with your fellow sisters. **Be authentic and who God created you to be!**

God has specially designed particular close relationships for you. He knows your makeup and character. We need to carefully choose our friends because they will affect us for good or for evil. A good strong Christian friend will love you and critique you. They will look for ways to help make you stronger. A friend or associate with strong character will encourage you. She will help you to maintain a good reputation even when it means disagreeing with you. A good friend understands that her reputation will improve yours, for you are known by the company you keep, (Thanks mom).

As a "Total Woman," we must choose our friends carefully and wholly be "sold out" to God!

"Let the Beauty of the Lord our God be upon us."

You are more precious than diamonds or rubies. I pray that you have examined areas of your life and made a decision to reflect

God's beauty through wholeness. I have shared my beauty secrets with you throughout these pages. Now allow that inner beauty to radiate from the inside out! Allow the sparkle in your eyes, the warmth of your smile, the kindness of your words, the poise of your stand, the grace in your walk, be adorned with compassion, and let the character of Christ reflect your Heavenly Father who has redeemed you through Christ.

Total Women, I encourage you to reinforce who you are every day! Say what God has said about you. Remember you are fearfully and wonderfully made, created in the image of the Almighty God. **Walk in His Wholeness! You are a "Total Woman!"**

One last word, permit me to leave with you a list of daily declarations that you can choose to confess. When used daily they will help you to continue to walk as a "Total Woman."

Your daily confessions

I am saved by grace.
I am redeemed by the blood.
I am free from condemnation.
I am a new creature in Christ.
I am crucified with Christ.
I am the righteousness of God.
I am loved by God.
I am the elect of God.
I am a part of the royal priesthood.
I am a joint heir with Jesus Christ.
I am complete in Him.
I am alive with Him.
I am living in Him, and He in me.
I am the temple of the Holy Spirit.
I am filled with the Holy Spirit.
I am victorious through Christ.
I am born on purpose with a purpose.
I am a visionary. I have vision.
I am who God says I am.
I am more than a conqueror.
I am an overcomer.
I am protected by the angels in heaven.
I am a partaker of His divine nature.
I am called of God.
I am the head and not the tail.
I am above and not beneath.
I am created in His image.
I am empowered to defeat the enemy.
I am empowered to decree a thing and it
shall be established.
I am the apple of God's eye.
I am fearfully and wonderfully made.
I am value to God and myself and family.
I am renewed in my mind.
I am spiritually whole.
I am physically whole.
I am a **TOTAL WOMAN!**

About the Author

Carolyn Hunt is the founder of Carolyn Hunt Ministries and co-founder and pastor of *Walk In The Word Family Church* in Monroe, Louisiana. Her heart is filled with compassion as she faithfully fulfills the assignment and purpose of God for her life.

Carolyn hosts The Total Women's Conference each year to help others to discover their purpose and live out their destiny! Thousands are empowered to not just live, but to live on purpose. Her graceful style of preaching has opened doors for her throughout the World to teach and preach the uncompromised gospel. Her teachings are prophetic, pungent and powerful.

Carolyn travels the nation ministering the Gospel, and watching lives changed and set free, spiritually, physically and socially. She is humbled by the call to heal broken hearts, transform lives and save souls.

She is a wife, mother and grandmother. She and her husband are the proud parents of one daughter, two granddaughters, four grandsons and many spiritual sons and daughters.

Other Books and Teaching CD's and DVD's by Carolyn Hunt

Books
A New Walk
Is Something Missing?
Issues of The Heart

CD's and DVD's
Just Do Something
Unordinary Faith
Issues of The Heart
Journey To Destiny
Are you expecting it?
Be Determined to Be Determined
Adversity For a Greater Purpose
Achieving Your Purpose
Change Your Mind
In the Meantime
Dealing with Distractions
Help for Discouragement
How to Conquer Doubt
A hole in a Whole
Shut The Door
If Only – No Regrets
My Mind is Made Up
The Greatest Treasure
Spirit of Offense
Empowered to Impact
Confront it to Conquer it!
It's Time to Mount Up
My Situation is Not my Destiny

To contact the author

Please write our offices at:
Carolyn Hunt Ministries
Walk in the Word Church
P.O. Box 7149
Monroe, Louisiana 71211

Or call:
(318) 410-0546
Or 877-410-0546

Email:
chuntministries@bellsouth.net
www.carolynhuntministries.org
www.walkinthewordfamilychurch.org
www.thetotalwoman.org
Visit her on
YouTube
Facebook

CAROLYN HUNT MINISTRIES

the

TOTAL

Woman

SPIRIT · SOUL · BODY

1 THESSALONIANS 5:23

THE TOTAL WOMAN

YOU WERE CREATED TO REFLECT HIS BEAUTY!

In this dynamic book, *"The Total Woman"* you'll discover how you can be complete and whole in every area of your life.

This is a book for and about women – women who desire to discover:
- Who they are
- What God has designed and desired for them to be
- What are the principals and qualities of becoming a *"Total Woman"*
- What is your purpose in life?

Dr. Carolyn Hunt writes out of her own unique experience to help women from all walks of life to be confident in whom God designed them to be.

The Total Woman features inspiring words to take women on a journey from brokenness to wholeness. This book will motivate women to cease to complain and compare themselves to others, and commence to search for the hidden woman which regulates her life.

The time is now! It's time to step out from under your hidden self and step into your God ordained identity. God designed us…He created us whole… in the image of the Most High God. We are fearfully and wonderfully made!

Dr. Hunt is founder of Carolyn Hunt Ministries and pastor of Walk in the Word Family Church in Monroe, Louisiana. Carolyn travels the nation ministering the Gospel, and watching lives changed and set free, spiritually, physically and socially. She is humbled by the call to heal broken hearts, transform lives and save souls.